Simple and Practical

Accounting

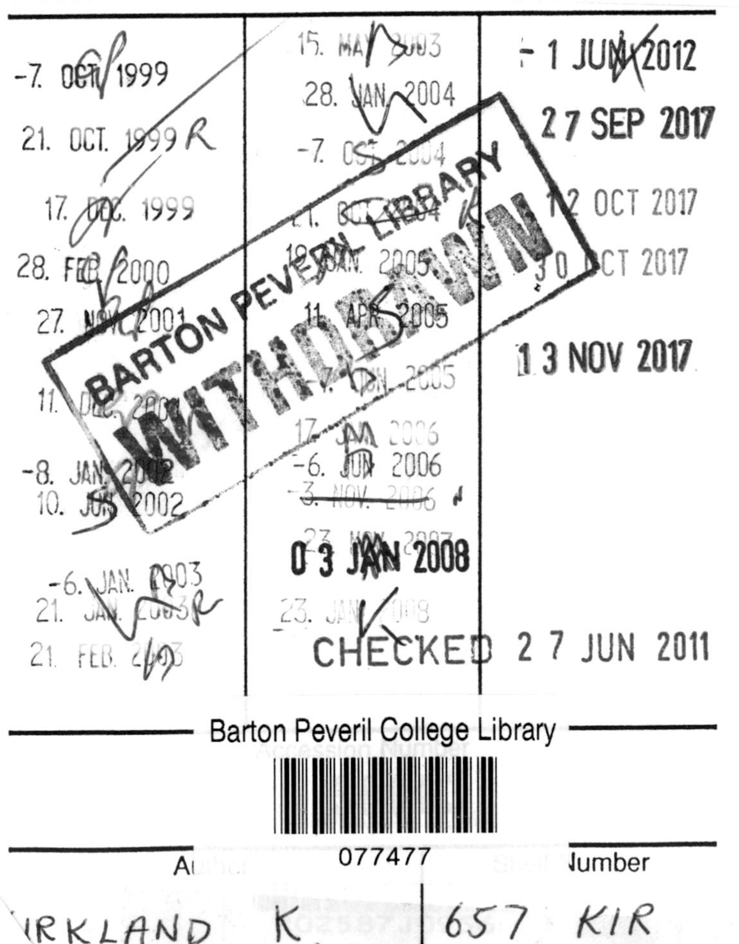

Simple and Practical

Accounting

A Guide to Understanding Accounts and Accounting Terms

Keith Kirkland and Stuart Howard

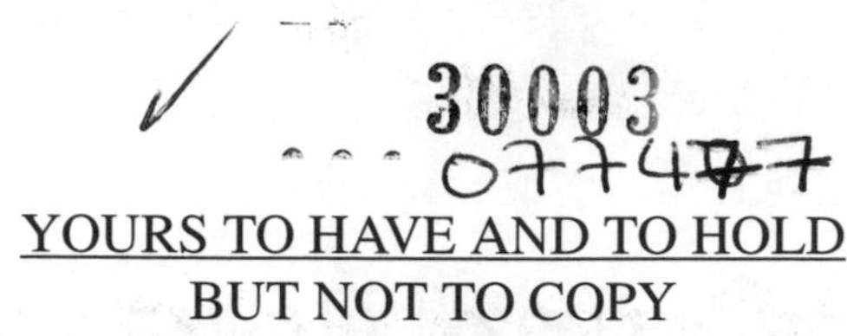

First published in 1998

Kogan Page Limited
120 Pentonville Road
London N1 9JN

Illustrations by John Loader

British Library Cataloguing in Publication Data

A CIP record for this book is available from the British Library

ISBN 0 7494 2929 1

Typeset by Vector Business Development.
Printed and bound in Great Britain by Bell & Bain Ltd, Glasgow.

Contents

Part 1 – Annual Accounts

Chapter 1

Introduction

Everyone Can Understand Accounts!

Contrary to popular belief, it isn't hard to understand accounts. Once you understand the basic principles, most of accounting is common sense. In this book, we start at the beginning assuming that you have no previous accounting knowledge. We will build a picture of accounting, which enables you to cut through accounting jargon. The contents of this book won't make you into a qualified accountant. You will, however, be able to have an informed discussion with one!

Accounting Basics

Accounting breaks down into three broad areas. These are:

- Book-keeping
- Annual Accounts
- Management Accounts.

Let's have a look at each of these areas in a little more detail.

Book-keeping

Book-keeping collects together information about the business and organises it. Book-keeping is *very* important – if you don't have good 'books', you can't have good accounts! Most manual book-keeping records cash in and cash out in an analysed cashbook. In this book, we show you how to convert your manual cashbooks into a set of accounts. Manual book-keeping is covered in more detail in another book in the series called *Simple and Practical Book-keeping*. Computerised book-keeping is covered in a different book called *Accounting with Computers*.

Annual Accounts

As the name suggests, Annual Accounts are produced once a year. These accounts normally comprise a profit and loss account and balance sheet. They are usually drawn up by an accountant or auditor appointed by the business. The profit and loss account tells you how much profit the business earned in the previous year. The balance sheet tells you how much the business is worth.

Annual accounts are principally used to:

- calculate the amount of tax owed by the business to the Inland Revenue
- notify the owners/shareholders of the business whether the business made a profit or loss
- provide evidence of trading performance to outside lenders such as banks, HP companies, business creditors etc.

Annual accounts are covered in the first part of this book. This part will be useful to people who want to understand accounting terminology. It provides an appreciation of how profit and loss accounts and balance sheets are structured.

Management Accounts

Management accounts serve a completely different purpose to annual accounts. Management accounts provide information for the managers *within* the business. You cannot use the annual accounts for day-to-day management because:

- They arrive too late. By the time your annual accounts are available, you could be well into the new financial year. Much could have changed. How do you know whether the business is still trading profitably?

- Annual accounts don't contain sufficient detail for management control, they are a broad summary of last year's events. You need more detailed information to run the business. Management information should be available as and when it happens.

Management accounts are mainly about budgets. Budgeting involves:

- planning what you want to happen in the coming year
- checking on progress (usually on a monthly basis)
- acting when things get out of hand.

Budgets are generally controlled on two documents. These are the cash flow forecast and the profit plan.

Although businesses need a cash plan and a profit plan, financial reporting rarely stops there. In addition, most businesses need special reports on key areas such as debtors, creditors, stock, wages etc. These are called key management reports. Management accounting is dealt with in the second part of this book.

Chapter 2

The Accounting Ground Rules

Accounts are put together and read by all sorts of people. It makes sense, therefore, to have some common ground rules which everyone adheres to. These common standards are overseen by an organisation called the Accounting Standards Board. This is a committee comprised of representatives of the major accounting bodies in the UK and the Republic of Ireland. The Accounting Standards Board issues directives which ensure that accounts present a 'true and fair view' of the businesses they describe. If you want to know more detail about accounting standards in the future, you will find a reference to it in Appendix 4. However, you don't need this detail now to follow the rest of the book. Let's now briefly introduce the fundamental accounting concepts.

Fundamental Accounting Concepts

Accounts are expected to present a 'true and fair' view of the business they describe. Indeed, every time a business is audited, the auditers have to sign a statement certifying that the accounts do indeed present a true and fair view. Accountants have some basic guidelines which help them decide whether accounts do present a true and fair view. These are called the fundamental accounting concepts. The following concepts should be applied to every set of accounts.

The Going Concern Concept

This means that the business is economically viable. Neither the profit and loss account nor the balance sheet show that it will be necessary to liquidate the business in the foreseeable future.

The Accruals Concept

Income and expenditure are adjusted so that they appear in the accounts at the time the income is earned or the expenditure incurred, not when the money is actually received or paid. Here are a couple of examples to make things clearer.

Suppose that we sell goods on credit. The sale is taken into the accounts when the customer receives the goods, not when they actually pay for them. The sale transaction is deemed to take place when ownership changes, this is not necessarily the same time as the cash is received.

Here is another example. Suppose we manufacture items for sale. The cost of the materials used to make those items is charged to the profit and loss account in the period when they are used, not at the time the materials were originally bought.

Don't worry if this is difficult to grasp as we will return to this topic many times later in the book.

The Consistency Concept

This concept assumes that there is consistency in accounting treatment from one period to the next. This is important because a change of accounting basis (like the method of valuing stock, for example) could cause a significant distortion in profit which would mislead readers of the accounts. If there *must* be a change of accounting treatment for one period to the next, it should be clearly stated in the accounts.

The Prudence Concept

Put simply, this means that accountants like all surprises to be happy ones! In practical terms, it means you do not anticipate income and profit in a reckless manner. On the other hand, expenses and losses are incorporated even if you can only make an estimate of what those costs or losses are likely to be.

Chapter 3

The Profit and Loss Account

In this section, we introduce the notion of 'profit'. We will also look at some practical examples of profit and loss accounts.

Let's begin with a question.

Question

If you subtracted the amount of cash spent by your business in a year from the amount of cash received by your business in that year, would the difference represent your profit for the year? In other words does:

	Cash Received
less	Cash Spent
equal	Profit?

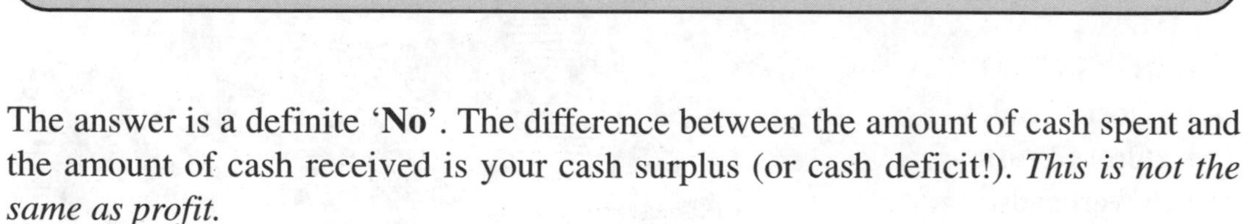

The answer is a definite '**No**'. The difference between the amount of cash spent and the amount of cash received is your cash surplus (or cash deficit!). *This is not the same as profit.*

Profit is a notional surplus arising from trading. It is notional because it does not just take cash into account, it makes additional adjustments for non-cash items such as:

- depreciation
- changing stock levels
- credit given to customers
- credit taken from suppliers.

The profit and loss account also apportions bills which span two accounting periods so that each period bears a fair share of the cost.

First we will have a look at the layout of the profit and loss account, then we will see how to calculate the figures.

What is a Profit and Loss Account?

A profit and loss account is a document which tells you whether the business is *trading* profitably. The word 'trading' is important since only income and expenditure connected with 'trading' appear in the profit and loss account. If you want to see *all* sources of income and *all* sources of expenditure, you have to look at something else called the 'cash flow statement'. This is explained in Chapter 9. Accountants do not normally produce cash flow statements for sole traders or partnerships as part of their annual accounts.

The profit and loss account summarises trading income and expenditure under five headings which are:

- Sales
- Cost of Sales
- Gross Profit
- Overheads
- Net Profit.

Profit

You can see from the illustration below that a profit and loss account is a simple five line equation. Gross profit is the difference between 'sales' and 'cost of sales'. Net profit is calculated by subtracting overheads from gross profit. This means that a 'bare bones' profit and loss account would look as follows:

	Sales
less	Cost of Sales
equals	Gross Profit
less	Overheads
equals	Net Profit

Let's have a look at each heading in a little more detail.

Sales

This is:

- the value of goods despatched to customers, or
- the value of services performed for customers.

Sales income is income strictly derived from normal trading activities.

It excludes income from unusual transactions of a capital nature such as sales of premises or sales of capital equipment. The sales line must only comprise sales income due to trading. Other transactions distort the underlying profitability of the business. Consistency in sales recording facilitates comparisons between each year's performance.

Loss

Cost of Sales

These are costs *directly* associated with providing the goods or services sold. Cost of sales will normally comprise materials consumed, operational labour and expenses directly asociated with producing the sales. These are explained below.

Materials Cost

Let's work out the cost of stock sold for a retailer. The stock cost could be found by taking the cost of all items sold individually and then adding them together. In practice, the labour involved in recording the cost price of every item sold would be immense.

We need some form of short-cut calculation which enables the shopkeeper to infer the cost of stock without actually checking every item. This is done by taking the stock value at the beginning of a trading period and adding the value of goods bought (called 'purchases'). You subtract the amount of stock remaining at the end of the trading period as follows:

	Opening Stock
plus	Purchases
	Stock Available for Sale
less	Closing Stock
equals	Cost of Stock Sold

Obviously, the cost of sales figure calculated in this way is subject to some fairly major assumptions. These assumptions include, for example, that:

- the stock check was conducted accurately
- a consistent method of valuing stock has been chosen
- all goods paid for have actually been received
- the count for opening and closing stock was accurate.

We need to be sure that the cost of sales figure is matched to the figure for sales. If 'cost of sales' and 'sales' referred to differing volumes of goods (or services) then the gross profit margin calculation would be misleading.

Labour and Expense

Labour and expenses included in 'cost of sales' must be *directly* associated with the sale, otherwise they are included in overheads. Continuing with our retailer example, the sales assistants' wages will be included in 'cost of sales'. The shop manager's salary, however, would not be included in cost of sales since he is not directly making the sale. The manager's salary would normally be included in overheads. In general terms, therefore, cost of sales is the amount spent in providing the goods (or service) directly, which are subsequently sold to customers.

Gross Profit

This is simply the difference between the 'sales' and 'cost of sales' figures.

Overheads

These are expenses which are *not* directly related to the amount of goods sold. They tend to be fixed over quite wide ranges of output. They comprise, for example, management salaries, depreciation, rent, rates, interest charges, administration costs and sales administration.

Net Profit

This is the result when you subtract the overheads from the gross profit. Here is an example of the layout for a simple profit and loss account where the five main headings have been expanded to include a little more detail.

		£	£
	Sales		**1000**
	Opening Stock	400	
add	Purchases	800	
		1200	
less	Closing Stock	575	
	Cost of Stock Sold	625	
	Manual Labour	100	
	Expense	25	
	Cost of Sales		**750**
	Gross Profit		**250**
	Overheads		
	Rent	50	
	Rates	10	
	Admin Labour	90	
	Depreciation	10	**160**
	Net Profit		**90**

Bodgit the Builder Example

Let's have a look at an example. We will put together a profit and loss account for an imaginary business called Bodgit the Builder. The final profit and loss account is shown on pages 30 and 31. Each time you calculate an entry, turn to pages 30 and 31 to see how it appears on the finished profit and loss account. We have assumed that Bodgit keeps his books manually in an analysed cashbook. We will adjust the cash entries in his cashbook to produce the profit and loss figures for the business.

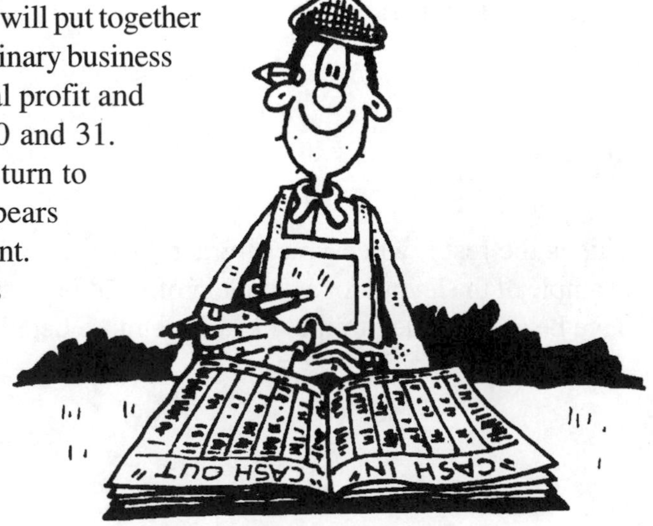

Sales

Like many small businesses, Mr Bodgit keeps his books on a cash basis. If Bodgit didn't give credit to his customers, the 'sales' figure in the profit and loss account would be the amount of cash received during the trading year. However, Bodgit does offer his customers credit. Because of this, we have to make a few alterations to the cash received figure. Here is the reason. You may remember that, according to the accruals principle, the sale is deemed to take place when ownership changes hands. In practical terms, this is usually the date when the invoice is raised. Since customers don't pay their bills until some time after they receive the invoice, you have to adjust the 'cash received from sales' figure to reflect the outstanding debt. This is how you do it.

Adjust the 'cash received from sales' figure as follows.

Subtract cash received during *this* trading year which relates to goods or services sold in the *previous* trading year. This is easy to do provided that we record the outstanding debtors at the end of every trading year.

Add cash owed at the end of this trading year. Although we haven't received the money, we should include these transactions as part of this year's 'sales'. The cash owed to the business is, of course, the sales debtors figure on the last day of the trading year.

These adjustments only apply if you record sales as cash receipts. If you have a computerised accounting system, you will find that the sales ledger program automatically calculates the correct sales figure for you based on the date that the invoice was raised.

Here is an example of the adjustments required where businesses record their sales as 'cash received from sales'.

Example

- Your financial year ended on 30 April 1996
- Your opening sales debtors were £6,000 (on 1 May 1995)
- Your closing sales debtors were £8,000 (on 30 April 1996)
- Cash received from sales during the year was £50,000

What sales figure will you put into your profit and loss account?

If you do not adjust your profit and loss account for sales debtors, your accounts will show sales of: **£50000**

If you adjust your profit and loss account for sales debtors, you will show sales of:

	Cash received in the year	50000	
less	Sales debtors at 1 May 1995	(6000)	
		44000	
add	Sales debtors at 30 April 1996	8000	
Your accounts will now show sales of			**£52000**
			£2000

You will see that sales debtors are deducted at the beginning of the year and added at the end of the year. This reflects the sales that you actually made in the year, *irrespective of whether you have received payment for the sales or not.* Note that the sales figure shown on the profit and loss account between pages 30 and 31 appears as £53,000 not £52,000. This is because the sales figure also incorporates a work-in-progress adjustment of £1,000 which is explained below.

Work-in-Progress Adjustments

This adjustment affects businesses which make or build things. Work-in-progress is partly manufactured work which is not yet in a state in which it will be accepted by a customer. People who make things often hold stocks of part-finished work. Once again, you need to know:

- the amount of work-in-progress at the beginning of the trading period, and
- the amount of work-in-progress at the end of the trading period.

This enables you to adjust the profit figure for work-in-progress distortions. Here is an example.

Work-in-Progress Example

Imagine that you are a builder building an extension for a customer for £4000

- Your financial year ended on 30 April 1996
- You started the extension on 1 March 1996
- So far you have spent £2,000 on labour and materials
- Opening work-in-progress at 1 May 1995 was £1,000
- Closing work-in-progress at 30 April 1996 was £2,000

Continued overleaf

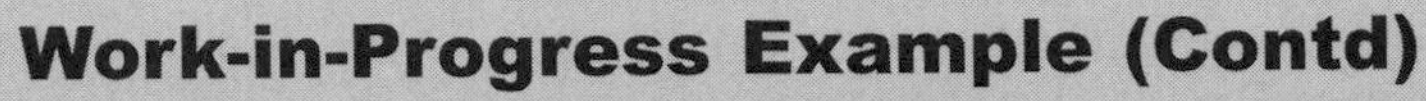

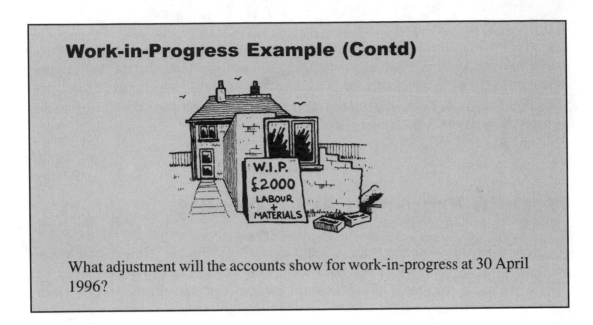

Work-in-Progress Example (Contd)

What adjustment will the accounts show for work-in-progress at 30 April 1996?

This adjustment is normally made via the sales figure. We will use the same sales figure as we calculated on page 14, ie £52,000.

If you do not adjust your profit and loss account for work in progress, your accounts will show sales of			**£52000**
If you adjust your profit and loss account for work in progress, your accounts will show sales of:			
	Sales in the year	52000	
less	Work-in-progress as at 1 May 1995	(1000)	
		51000	
add	Work-in-progress at 30 April 1996	2000	
The accounts will show sales of			**£53000**
			£1000

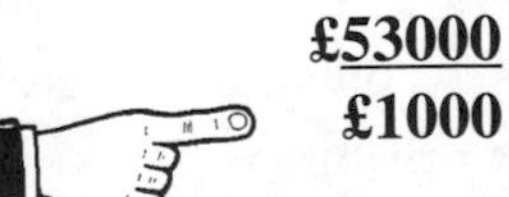

Your accounts have now been adjusted for work-in-progress. Remember, this adjustment generally applies to businesses which manufacture their own products. It does not apply to businesses which buy in the finished product for resale.

Cost of Sales

These are costs *directly* associated with providing the goods or services sold during the year (hence their alternative name of 'direct costs'). Bodgit builds houses, garages and extensions. This incurs costs such as building labour, building materials, diesel and petrol. The 'cost of sales' figure is made up of labour, materials and expense.

We need to make several adjustments to our cash records before they can be used in the profit and loss account. These adjustments include:

- credit taken on purchases
- stock adjustments.

Credit Taken on Purchases

Bodgit receives credit from his suppliers. This means he receives his goods and services before he pays the bill. Legally, however, the transaction should be shown in the accounts at the time when the goods or services are *accepted,* not on the date that payment is made.

Since Bodgit keeps his records on a cash paid basis, he will have to adjust the cash purchases figure in his books to bring his records onto an accrual basis. This is how he does it.

Some suppliers will have sent Bodgit invoices which he had not paid at the end of his current financial year. The value of these outstanding invoices has to be added to the cash figure. On the other hand, some cash payments made in the current financial year will be for goods delivered in the previous financial year. These payments need to be *subtracted* from the cash out figure for this year. Here is an example of how to make the adjustment.

Cost of Sales Example – Purchase Creditors

- Your financial year ended on 30 April 1996
- Your opening creditors (on 1 May 1995) were £4,000
- Your closing creditors (on 30 April 1996) were £5,250
- You paid £40,000 cash for purchases in the year

What figure for purchases would you put into your profit & loss account?

If you do not adjust your profit and loss account for purchase creditors then your accounts will show purchases of **£40000**

If you do adjust your profit and loss account for purchase creditors, your accounts will show purchases of:

	Purchases paid for in the year	40000
less	Purchase creditors at 1 May 1995	(4000)
		36000
add	Purchase creditors at 30 April 1996	5250

Your accounts will show purchases of **£41250**

SEE THE DIFFERENCE **£1250**

You can see that the accounts now reflect the true purchases in the year, whether you have paid for them or not.

Remember that the adjustments shown above are only important if you rely on manual accounting using a cashbook. If you run a computerised accounting system, the 'purchase ledger' is based on transaction dates, not on payment dates. This means that the computer automatically supplies the 'correct' figure for purchases received.

We now need to make a further adjustment for stock.

Stock Adjustments

If you sell items from stock this year which you bought in a previous trading year, you will artificially inflate your profit for this year. This is because you will be showing the income this year and the corresponding expenditure in the previous year. This creates a misleading profit fluctuation. To eliminate these misleading profit calculations caused by changing stock levels, we need to know two things:

- How much stock did I have at the beginning of the year?
- How much stock did I have at the end of the trading year?

From these two figures, we can work out the stock used during the year. Here is an example.

Stock Example

- Your financial year ended on 30 April 1996
- Your stock at the beginning of the year (1 May 1995) was £3,000
- Your stock at the end of the year (30 April 1996) was £3,500
- The stock adjustment is usually made via your purchases figure (remember the adjusted purchases figure above for the year was £41,250)

If you do not adjust your profit and loss account for stock, your accounts will show purchases of **£41250**

If you do adjust your profit and loss accounts for stock, your accounts will show purchases of:

	Purchases	41250
add	Stock at 1 May 1995	3000
		44250
less	Stock at 30 April 1996	(3500)

The accounts will now show purchases of **£40750**

SEE THE DIFFERENCE **£500**

Your accounts have now been adjusted for stock.

A Note on Stock Valuation

We have shown how changes in stock levels are incorporated into the profit calculation. But how do you value stock? Stock can be valued in one of several ways. Your accountant will require you to value stock at the lesser of cost price or net realisable value.

- 'Cost price' is the price you paid for the stock (excluding value added tax).
- 'Net realisable value' is the amount you would expect to realise if you sold the stock (excluding value added tax). You need to deduct the cost of arranging the sale. You would use this figure if you had obsolete stock which could only be sold at a price below what you paid for it.

Never value stock at its retail selling price. If you do, you will include profit in your accounts which you have not yet earned. This would violate the 'prudence' concept.

Gross Profit

This is derived by subtracting the 'cost of sales' figure from the 'sales' figure.

	Sales
less	Cost of Sales
equals	Gross Profit

The gross profit is an important measure of trading success. Without a good gross profit, you can never have a good net profit. Typical gross profit figures for different businesses are shown in Appendix 2 on page 191. Gross profit can be expressed as a percentage of sales turnover.

This is calculated as:

$$\text{Gross Profit Percent} = \frac{\text{Gross Profit x 100}}{\text{Sales}}$$

For example, if a builder's gross profit was below average, it could be because he was paying too much for his materials, paying too much for labour or selling his building work too cheaply.

Overheads

Overheads comprise all expenditure not included in cost of sales. Overheads are sometimes called 'indirect costs'. Overheads comprise the non producing part of the business. For example, they include office rent and rates, office salaries, insurance, delivery charges etc. Sales salaries are overheads for all businesses except retail. This is because these employees do not usually produce the product or perform the service for the customer directly.

Generally speaking, overheads tend to be time related rather than volume related. For example, if you rent your business premises for £10,000 per annum, you will still pay £10,000 irrespective of whether you sell one pounds worth of business or 50,000 pounds worth of business in that year.

There are three aspects to overheads which warrant further attention, these are:

- prepayments
- accruals
- depreciation.

Prepayments

What are prepayments? A prepayment occurs when you pay *in advance* for goods and services which you have not yet received. You make prepayments for items such as insurance premiums, rent and rates.

Let's take an imaginary example. Suppose an insurance premium of £1,200 was paid on 31 December 1995. If your financial year ends on 30 April 1996. Your prepayment can be calculated from the following illustration.

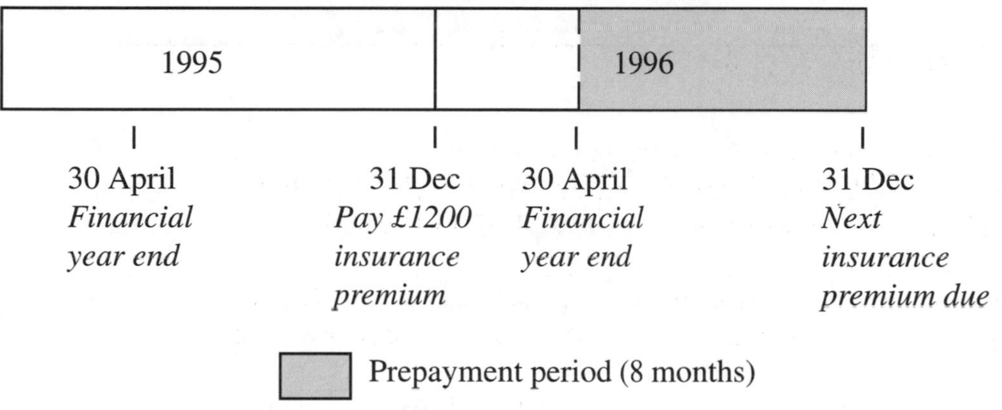

Your financial year ends on 30 April 1996 so you have only 'used' four months of your premium by the end of your financial year. You will have 'unused' premium covering a further eight months. This will be 'used' between 1 May 1996 and 31 December 1996.

The prepayment shown in the profit and loss account at 30 April 1996 (the financial year end) will be 8/12 of £1,200 which is £800.

Prepayments Example

Let's now develop the example. As with all the other adjustments to financial accounts, we need to consider the beginning of the year as well as the end of the year. Let's assume that last year's prepayment (which was used this year) was £500. We will make the adjustment for 1 May 1996 (which will be the start of our next financial year). The insurance premium cost £1,200.

If you do not adjust your profit and loss account for insurance premiums, your accounts will show insurance costs of **£1200**

If you do adjust your profit and loss account for prepayments, your insurance account in the profit and loss account will be:

	Prepayment existing at 1 May 1995	500
add	Insurance premium paid	1200
		1700
less	Prepayment at 30 April 1996	(800)

Your accounts will show **£900**

SEE THE DIFFERENCE **£300**

You have now adjusted the accounts for the insurance prepayment.

Accruals

These occur where we are billed *at the end* of a period (say, a quarter) for goods and services consumed during the quarter. Main examples are telephone, electricity and gas bills. Your accounts will need to show an estimate of the cost of telephone, electricity, gas etc consumed between the date of your last bill and your financial year end.

Let's work out an accrual for electricity assuming that your year end is 30 April 1996. The last bill that you paid, which was £300, covered the quarter to 31 March 1996. Therefore, you owe one month's electricity. We will assume that your next electricity bill will be similar, so our accrual would be one third of a quarter's bill which is one third of £300, ie £100.

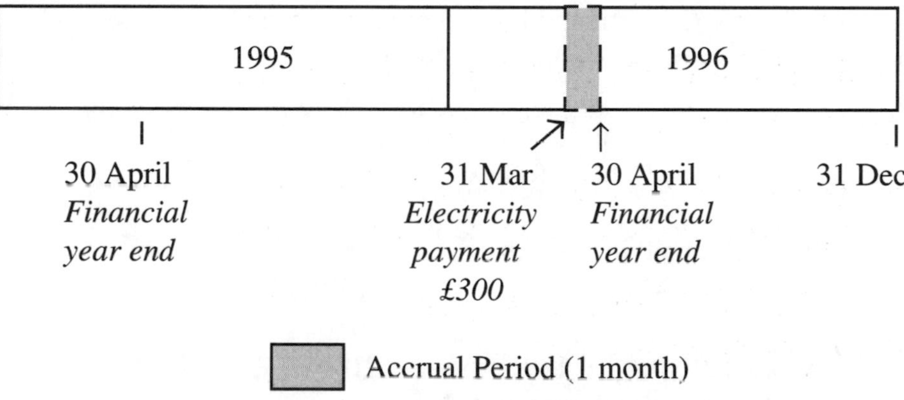

The following example shows how this adjustment is made in your accounts.

Accrual Example

Again we have to adjust for accruals at the beginning of the financial year as well as the end. Let's assume that the accrual for electricity at the start of your year, ie 1 May 1995 was £50. You have paid electricity in the year of £1,000.

Your accounts will be adjusted as follows:

If you do not adjust your profit and loss account for accruals, your electricity charge in the accounts will show **£1000**

If you do adjust your profit and loss account for accruals, your electricity account will be as follows:

	Electricity paid in the year	1000	
less	Accrual at 1 May 1995	(50)	
		950	
add	Accrual at 30 April 1996	100	
	Your electricity account will show		**£1050**
	SEE THE DIFFERENCE		**£50**

Your accounts have now been adjusted for the electricity accrual.

Depreciation

The cashbook will show money spent on the purchase of capital items such as cars, vans, office equipment, machinery, premises etc. However, the profit calculation does not charge the whole cost of the asset in the year of acquisition. Here is the reason. Suppose one year you decide to re-equip the business in a big way. Imagine that you bought plant equipment and vehicles etc. If you charged the whole of these equipment costs to the profit and loss account in the year of acquisition, you would make a huge loss that year. Subsequent years, however, would show exceptional profits because the whole of the expenditure would have been written off against that previous year. This distortion would make it impossible to make a meaningful comparison between one year's profit and another.

To provide a 'fairer' charge against each year's profits, you must spread the cost of the equipment over its expected life. For example, if a lorry cost £16,000 and had an eight year life, each year's profit and loss account would be charged with £2,000 of 'wear and tear' (assuming that the lorry had no scrap value). At the end of the eight year period, the value of the lorry in the firm's books would be nil. The lorry would have been 'paid for' out of the profits of the business during the time that the lorry was in use.

In the 'good old days' when businesses tended to replace like equipment with like, and there was very little inflation, this approach made a lot of sense. Today, however, inflation and technical change make the idea of depreciation based on historical costs a lot more suspect. Traditional depreciation techniques are likely to under-recover the cost of replacement assets. For the present, however, simply think of depreciation as the cost of wear and tear in any one year. We will return to the subject of depreciation in the next chapter.

Fully depreciated?

Depreciation Example

You buy an office computer for £2,000. It has an expected life of five years. There will be no scrap value. How much depreciation should you charge to this year's profit and loss account?

Your accounts will be adjusted as follows:

If you do not adjust your profit and loss account for depreciation, your accounts will show	**£2000**
If you do adjust your profit and loss account for depreciation, your accounts will show:	
$\frac{\text{Cost of Equipment}}{\text{Life}} = \frac{£2000}{5}$ pa	**£400**

You will see that the charge in the profit and loss account is £400 not £2000. The difference of £1,600 is carried forward and depreciated over the next four years. Your accounts have now been adjusted for depreciation.

Net Profit

The net profit is the final figure in the profit and loss calculations. It is often referred to as the 'bottom line'. You can now see why profit is *not* the amount of cash left in the till at the end of the trading period. Profit is a notional gain or loss after making the adjustments shown above.

It would be unwise to spend all of the profit. You may not have it in the form of cash yet – much of it could still be lying in customer accounts waiting to be collected. In addition, every business needs to build a cash reserve as insurance against the accidents and disasters which, inevitably, lie in wait. You may need cash to replace equipment. You will also need cash to pay tax on your profits, so money must be kept back to meet the inevitable demands of the Inland Revenue.

To summarise then, the net profit has to meet a variety of demands including:

- paying owners their dividends or drawings
- paying tax
- re-investment back into the business
- providing a cushion against a rainy day.

A Note on VAT

If you are VAT registered, Value Added Tax is *not* included in your profit and loss account. A business acts as an unpaid tax collector for the government. At no point in the collection cycle does the VAT belong to the business. Any amount due to (or from) HM Customs and Excise is recorded on the balance sheet (see the next chapter of this book). However, there is an exception if you are *not* VAT registered, the costs in your profit and loss account will be VAT inclusive.

A Note on Personal Expenses

Personal expenses should not be included in the profit and loss account. All expenditure shown in the accounts must be wholly and exclusively for the purpose of business. If for any reason private expenses *have been* included in the profit and loss account, they must be compensated for in the tax computations (which we will look at later in this book). Owners' personal drawings must not be included in the profit and loss account. They are shown as a deduction on the balance sheet (see later).

Sales - Cost of Sales = Gross Profit

Sales *less* **Cost of Sales** *equals* **Gross Profit**

Overheads

Expenses

Depreciation

Depreciation £400

Depreciation £100

Depreciation £500

Trading and Profit and Loss Account for the Year ended 30/4/96

Trading Account

		£	£
	Sales		**53000**
less	**Cost of Sales**		**40750**
	Gross Profit		**12250**

Overheads

	£	£
Rates	750	
Insurance	900	
Electricity	1050	
Telephone	250	
Postage & Stationery	100	
Bank Charges	50	
Motor Expenses	800	
Accountancy	250	
Sundry Expenses	150	
Depreciation (Computer)	400	
Depreciation (Plant)	100	
Depreciation (Motor)	500	
		(5300)

Net Profit	**6950**

Summary

We have now covered the main adjustments which your accountant will make to your profit and loss account. Shown below is the profit and loss account which your accountant would prepare for you using the examples taken from this section. For comparison, the figures from your cash accounts are also shown.

	Your Cash Accounts will show		Your Annual Accounts will show	
	£	£	£	£
Sales	50000		53000	
Less **Purchases**	40000		40750	
Gross Profit		10000		12250
Overheads				
Insurance	1200		900	
Electricity	1000		1050	
Cost of computer	2000		-	
Computer depreciation	-			400
Total of other overheads	2950		2950	
(as per Bodgit P&L)		7150		5300
Net Profit		2850		6950

See how your net profit has changed! Your net profit has increased from £2,850 to £6,950, an increase of £4,100.

These examples have, we hope, demonstrated that profit is not simply the difference between 'cash in' and 'cash out'. The profit figure reflects adjustments for debtors, creditors, stock changes, work-in-progress, accruals, prepayments and depreciation.

We will do some more profit and loss examples in Chapter 4. Before doing so, we need to look at another document called the balance sheet. This is produced by your accountant at the same time as the profit and loss account.

Chapter 4

The Balance Sheet

What is a Balance Sheet?

A balance sheet is a summary of all the assets and liabilities of a business on a certain date. In a sense, it is a snapshot of the firm's financial position on one day of the year.

What is the Purpose of a Balance Sheet?

Balance sheets serve several purposes. They inform the owners of the company's worth. Comparison of balance sheets between one year and the next shows the amount and disposition of profits generated by the business. Indeed, some people regard balance sheets as the equivalent of milestones on a journey, the profit and loss account serving as a 'route map' between balance sheets.

Suppliers of goods and services will find their *customer's* balance sheets interesting. An examination of the balance sheet will reveal the liquidity of the customer's business. This will reflect the customer's ability to meet debts as they become due.

Money lenders such as banks, HP companies and leasing companies will also find other people's balance sheets interesting since it will help them decide the financial strength of the business they are lending to. This indicates whether they are likely to get their money back!

The tax man will also take an interest in the balance sheet. Most tax inspectors have a solid understanding of accounts. The balance sheet will help them to decide how reliable the profit and loss figure is likely to be. This, in turn, will decide how readily they accept the business accounts for tax purposes.

A balance sheet is a list of the assets and liabilities of the business. Let's have a look at these assets and liabilities. We will see how they are shown on a balance sheet.

On pages 46 and 47, you will see the balance sheet for Mr Bodgit drawn up on 30 April 1996. Notice that there are four main headings. These are:

- Fixed assets
- Current assets
- Current liabilities
- Owner's capital.

Let's look at these in a little more detail.

Fixed Assets

Fixed assets are items of capital equipment bought for retention and use. Examples include land, buildings, office equipment, cars, vans, plant, machinery etc. Provided that the business owns the asset then it is listed on the balance sheet. (Items which are rented or hired are not owned by the business so cannot appear on the balance sheet. In fact, they appear on someone else's balance sheet!)

Fixed Assets

When you first buy a fixed asset, it is shown on the balance sheet at cost. With time, however, the item will gradually lose value. This is because it wears out or it becomes technically obsolete.

This loss of value is called depreciation. Each year, assets are shown at a lower and lower value until, eventually, they have no value at all.

Property is the only exception to the normal pattern of depreciation. In ordinary circumstances, we expect to sell property for at least as much as we paid for it. This means that we would not normally show property at purchase price less depreciation. Instead, we periodically ask a valuer to estimate the property's worth. This value (be it higher or lower than the original purchase price) would be the valuation appearing on the balance sheet.

How would you estimate the value of a 'normal' depreciating fixed asset? One obvious solution would be to invite a professional valuer in each year and ask his opinion. Whilst this may well result in a very accurate valuation, it would be both expensive and time consuming. In practice, accountants use a short cut method to calculate this loss in value, it is called 'depreciation'.

Straight Line Depreciation

Previously, we looked at the example of a £16,000 lorry which depreciated to nothing over its eight year life. We said that the depreciation was £2,000 per annum (provided that the lorry had no scrap value). In this instance, we were using something called 'straight line depreciation'. It is called 'straight line depreciation' because, if you were to plot the value of the lorry every year of its life, it would form a straight line starting at £16,000 and ending at nil value.

Another example of straight line depreciation is shown on pages 36 – 37. In this instance, a lathe costing £2,000 depreciates to nothing over a five year life. The amount appearing in the 'book value' column will be shown on the balance sheet at the end of each year. For example, at the end of year 2, we would show the lathe as having a 'book value' of £1,200 on the balance sheet. At the end of the fifth year, it would disappear from the balance sheet altogether.

The value in the right hand column (£400 per annum) is charged to the profit and loss account. This is because the loss of value in any one year is seen as a cost to the business for that year.

Example

Suppose that you bought a lathe for £2,000. It is expected to have an operating life of five years. The value of the lathe at the end of each year would be:

	Book Value £	Dep'n charged to P&L A/c £
Cost of lathe (new)	2000	
Value after 1 year	1600	400
2 years	1200	400
3 years	800	400
4 years	400	400
5 years	Nil	400

You can see from the above example that the same amount of depreciation is written off each year. A graph of equipment value over time appears as a straight line. The graph of the book value for our lathe would look as follows:

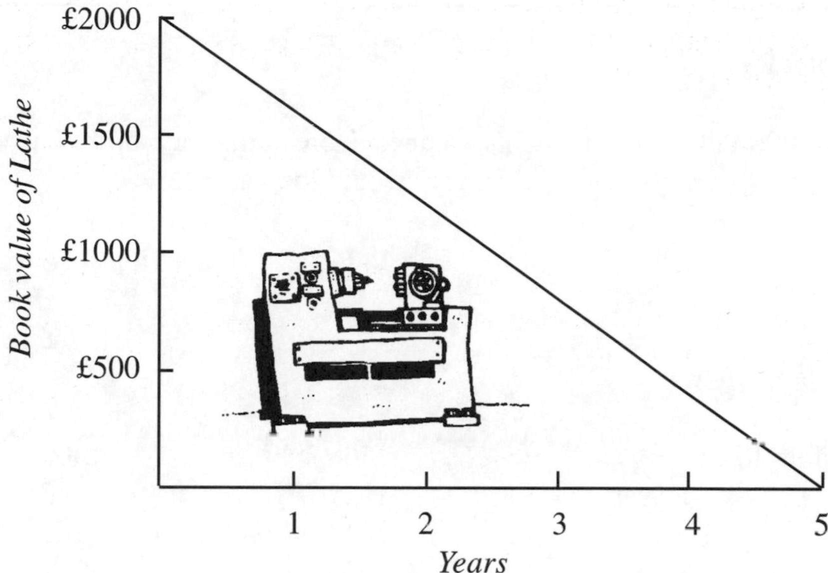

Sometimes, at the end of the anticipated life of the asset, we find that the asset still has some value. Any sum received on the sale of an asset over and above its book value is called a 'profit on disposal'.

If we anticipate that an asset will have a value at the end of its life (say as scrap value), we would draw our depreciation line from the value when new to the value for scrap. This would mean that we charged slightly less depreciation each year.

Reducing Balance Depreciation

For assets which lose most of their value in the early part of their life, we can use a different method of depreciation called the 'reducing balance' method. In this instance, the value of the asset falls by a fixed % every year.

Example

If our £2,000 lathe had a reducing balance depreciation rate of 25% per annum, its value at the end of each year would look as follows:

	Value	**Dep'n charged P&L A/c**
	£	£
Cost of lathe (new)	2000	
Value after 1 year	1500	500
2 years	1125	375
3 years	844	281
4 years	633	211
5 years	475	158

This can be shown graphically as follows.

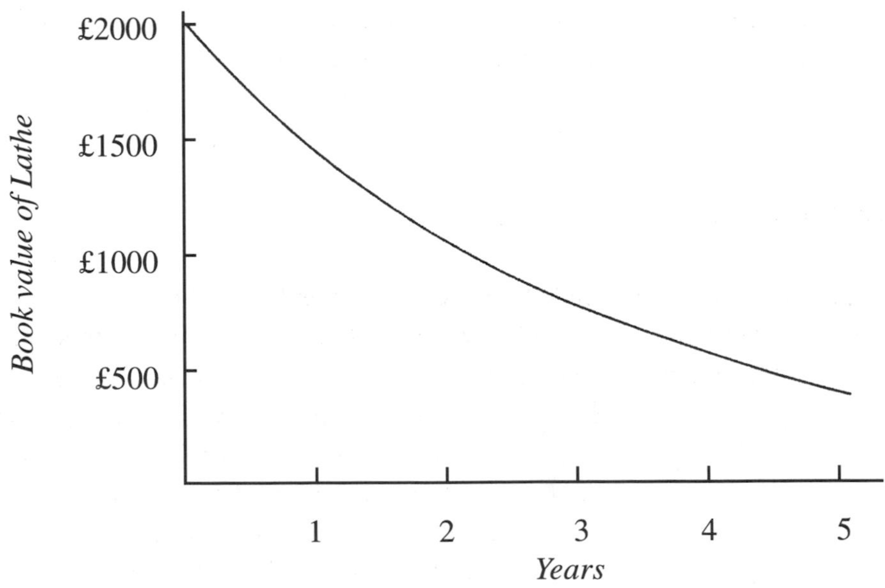

Look at the difference between the two methods! The reducing balance method has left us with a balance of £475 at the end of year 5. Depreciation under the reducing balance method can never quite reach zero.

Depreciation is treated as a cost to the business. Like all other costs, it is charged to the profit and loss account.

Depreciation is a way of retaining profit in the business. In theory, retaining the depreciation enables the business to fund the replacement of capital equipment. Under inflationary conditions, however, you would also need to retain additional profits. This is because when you replace the asset:

- inflation will mean that you have to pay more than you did originally
- you may replace the equipment with a technically enhanced product, which will probably cost more anyway.

Note If you turn to the balance sheet for Bodgit the Builder on pages 46 – 47, you will see that we have shown the depreciation for each fixed asset listed separately. We have done this to make the calculation clear. In practice, most accountants only show the 'book value' of the assets on the balance sheet. If you want to know the depreciation details, you need to turn to a supplementary page called a 'Schedule of Fixed Assets'. This document accompanies the profit and loss account and balance sheet in the accounts. Putting the detail on a separate schedule saves cluttering up the main accounts with detail.

How Does The Taxman View Depreciation?

Your depreciation calculation is completely ignored by the Inland Revenue for taxation purposes. Instead, the Revenue substitutes its own 'depreciation allowance' called a 'capital allowance'. This operates like the reducing balance method. It is normally based on a standard 25% 'depreciation' rate. We explain later how the taxman adjusts your profit, by substituting capital allowances for depreciation. For more details of capital allowances, see the *Simple and Practical Taxation* book in this series.

Current Assets

Current assets comprise items which:

- will eventually be sold to customers (eg stock), or
- cash, bank deposits and money owed to you by your customers.

Have a look at the sample balance sheet on pages 46 – 47. You will see that current assets for Bodgit comprise stock, work-in-progress, sales debtors, prepayments, bank balance and petty cash balance. Here are a few notes on each category.

Current Assets

Stock

Do you remember we said earlier that stock shown on the balance sheet is valued at the lesser of cost or net realisable value? Stock is important because it can tie up huge amounts of your cash. In addition to the purchase price, the business has to spend even more money paying for shelving, floorspace, storemen's wages and security to look after it! If your stock includes obsolete items, it may be worth selling them off, for whatever you can get, simply to release the space and save costs.

Work-in-Progress

This is the value you place on part-completed work which you cannot yet bill to customers. Work-in-progress is valued on the basis of cost incurred to date, not on the amount the customer will pay you eventually. This avoids anticipating a profit. Anticipating profit is not deemed to be 'prudent'! Many businesses have work-in-progress including manufacturers, builders, installers of equipment etc.

Sales Debtors

This is the value of outstanding debt owed to you by your customers. This can be a very significant item on the balance sheet. Uncontrolled debt can grow alarmingly. The older the debt, the less likely you are to collect the money! Credit control and debt collection is covered in another book in this series.

Prepayments

You may remember that certain bills are paid for 'up front'. Examples include insurance premiums, rent and rates. When we looked at the profit and loss account, we apportioned a part of these bills to the current financial year. The remainder of the bill will be charged to the next financial year. It is these prepayments which are recorded on the balance sheet as part of current assets.

Bank Account

If your bank balance is in credit, it will show as a current asset. If you are overdrawn then the overdraft will be shown as a current liability (explained later).

Cash/Petty Cash Balance

You may well be holding a small amount of cash or petty cash. Even if the cash value is small, it should still be entered as a current asset on the balance sheet.

Current Liabilities

These are the amounts that you owe your suppliers and other creditors. In the example on pages 46 – 47, we have shown purchase creditors, accruals and VAT owed. By the way, there is another name for current liabilities which is 'creditors under one year'. Let's have a look at some of these items in a little more detail.

Purchase Creditors

These are amounts owed to your normal trade creditors. It is important to monitor the amount of credit you have taken. This ensures that you are in a position to meet your bills as they become due.

A current liability

Accruals

We covered accruals when we looked at the profit and loss account in Chapter 3. We pay some of our bills such as telephone, electricity and gas etc in arrears. We estimate how much we owe our suppliers; this amount is due to them even though we haven't received the bill. At the financial year end, we add together all of our accruals and enter the total amount as a current liability on the balance sheet.

VAT due to HM Customs and Excise and other Taxes

It is easy to forget one of our major liabilities. This is VAT collected on behalf of HM Customs and Excise. Provided that we are not a net VAT reclaimer, we will normally owe something to HM Customs and Excise. Other tax liabilities could include arrears of National Insurance and PAYE if these remain unpaid on the date the balance sheet was drawn up.

Net Current Assets

Notice on pages 46 – 47 how our balance sheet shows the difference between current assets and current liabilities as a separate line called net current assets. The current assets add up to £24,400 and current liabilities add up to £6,850 which means that net current assets is the difference which is £17,550. This figure is very significant. If your current liabilities ever exceed your current assets, you could be in big financial trouble! In fact, conventional wisdom dictates that current assets should exceed current liabilities by a factor of about 2 to 1.

Don't wait until your accounts are produced to check whether you are solvent. It could be too late! Exercise control via your monthly (internal) management accounts, this is covered in Part 2 of this book. Keep a particular eye on the levels of current assets and current liabilities.

Current assets include the value of stock and work-in-progress. In practice, most people don't revalue their stock and work-in-progress on a monthly basis. However, you should *at least* check that the sum of your sales debtors plus bank account will enable you to pay your trade creditors and tax liabilities in the near future.

In our example on pages 46 – 47, we are in a very comfortable position. Our current liabilities only add up to £6,850 whilst we have £24,400 in current assets. Since £10,100 of our current assets are in the form of cash then we will have no problems paying our bills in the short term!

Total Net Assets

This represents the difference between all of the assets less all of the liabilities. In our case, the total net assets figure is £26,550. Notice how this figure is repeated at the bottom of the page under the heading of 'owners capital'.

If all of the assets and liabilities were shown at their 'market' value then this would represent the open market value of the business (excluding goodwill). In practice, many fixed assets may fetch less than their book value, so business valuations based on balance sheet values are highly suspect.

Owners Capital

If we subtract the total liabilities from the total assets on the balance sheet, we could deduce that the 'book value' of the business is £26,550. Let's see how this value arises.

Owners Capital Account

		£
	Balance brought forward from previous year	25600
Add	Net profit for the year	6950
		32550
Less	Private drawings	6000
	Balance carried forward to next year	26550

Providing the business has been trading for more than one year, there will always be a balance brought forward from last year's balance sheet. This brought forward amount represents the value of the business at the end of the previous year. Your accountant will add the net profit from your profit and loss account for the current year to your 'brought forward' value. From this total, you can see that he will deduct your private drawings. The resulting balance of £26,550 is carried forward into your next financial year.

Owners Capital

Summary

- The balance sheet is a statement of the assets and liabilities of your business at a given time.
- Assets are the things the business owns.
- Assets are divided into fixed assets and current assets.
- Liabilities are the amounts owed to others.
- Net current assets is the difference between current assets and current liabilities.
- Net current assets is sometimes called 'working capital'.
- The difference between total assets and total liabilities is the owner's 'capital employed' in the business.

We have now completed this chapter. In the next chapter, we will attempt some examples. These will enable you to prepare a simple profit and loss account and balance sheet for yourself.

Fixed Assets

Current Assets

Current Liabilities

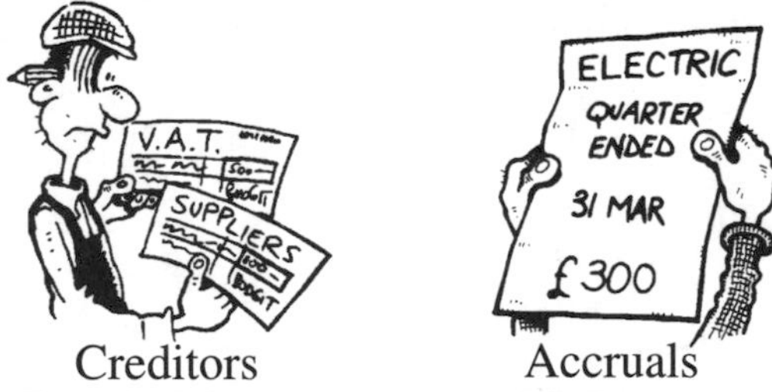

Balance Sheet as at 30/4/96

Fixed Assets

	B/Fwd	Depn	Value	
	£	£	£	
Property – Builders Yard	2000	-	2000	
Motor Vehicles	5000	(500)	4500	
Plant & Machinery	1000	(100)	900	
Computer	2000	(400)	1600	
				9000

Current Assets

Stock	3500		
Work-in-Progress	2000		
Sales Debtors	8000		
Prepayments – Insurance	800		
Bank Account Balance	10000		
Petty Cash Balance	100		
		24400	

Current Liabilities

Purchase Creditors	5250		
Accruals – Electricity	100		
VAT due to HMC&E	1500		
		6850	
Net Current Assets			**17550**

Total Net Assets **26550**

Owners Capital

Represented by:		
Mr Bodgit Capital Account	2500	
Balance B/fwd Previous Year	6950	
Net Profit for the Year	32550	
Less Private Drawings	(6000)	
Balance C/Fwd		**26550**

Chapter 5

Build Your Own Set of Accounts

In this chapter, we will build a profit and loss account and then a balance sheet. You will need to refer to the notes in Chapters 3 and 4 to help you complete this example.

The Profit and Loss Account

Our profit and loss account involves calculations for sales debtors, stock, work-in-progress, prepayments, accruals and depreciation. Look at the profit and loss account answer sheet on page 56. Enter your answers on this page as you proceed through this section. Our financial year started on 1 May 1995 and finished on 30 April 1996.

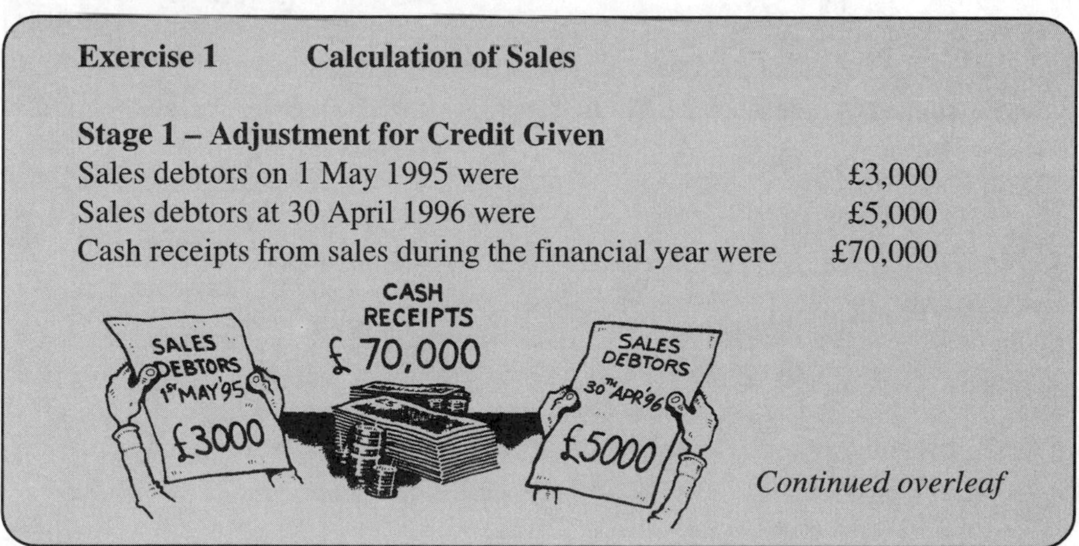

Exercise 1 Calculation of Sales

Stage 1 – Adjustment for Credit Given

Sales debtors on 1 May 1995 were	£3,000
Sales debtors at 30 April 1996 were	£5,000
Cash receipts from sales during the financial year were	£70,000

Continued overleaf

Exercise 1 (Contd)

Calculate sales for the year using the headings below:

	Cash Received from sales in the year	
less	Sales debtors at 1 May 1995	
	Difference	
add	Sales debtors at 30 April 1996	
	Sales adjusted for credit	

Do not transfer this figure to your profit and loss account yet as we now need to make an adjustment for work-in-progress.

Stage 2 – Adjustment for Work-In-Progress

Work-in-progress at 1 May 1995 was £6,500

Work-in-progress at 30 April 1996 was £8,200

Calculate the adjusted sales figure starting with your answer from Stage 1:

	Sales adjusted for credit	
less	Work-in-progress at 1 May 1995	
	Difference	
add	Work-in-progress at 30 April 1996	
	Sales per the accounts	

Check your answer with the model on page 175. Transfer this answer to the sales line of your profit and loss pro-forma on page 56.

Exercise 2 Purchases

Stage 1 – Adjustment for Creditors

Purchases creditors at 1 May 1995	£8,000
Purchases creditors at 30 April 1996	£9,200
Cash purchases paid for in the year	£55,000

Calculate your purchases for the year ended 30 April 1996 by inserting the amounts above:

	Purchases paid for in the year	
less	Purchase creditors at 1 May 1995	
	Difference	
add	Purchases creditors at 30 April 1996	
	Purchases adjusted for credit	

Check your answer with the model answer on page 176 but do not transfer the result to your profit and loss account yet. We need to make a further adjustment in Stage 2 to cover stock changes.

Exercise 2 (Contd)

Stage 2 Adjustment for Stock Changes

Opening stock at 1 May 1995 was £5,000

Closing stock at 30 April 1996 was £6,000

Start with your 'purchases adjusted for credit' answer from Stage 1

	Purchases from Stage 1	56,200
add	Stock at 1 May 1995	5 000
		61 200
less	Stock at 30 April 1996	6000
	Purchases per accounts	55 200

Check your answer with the model on page 176. Transfer this value to the 'Cost of Sales' (Purchases) line on your profit and loss account on page 56. You can now calculate the gross profit figure (also on page 56) by subtracting the value of 'cost of sales' from 'sales'.

Exercise 3 Prepayments

An insurance premium of £2,400 was paid during the year which covered the period 1 November 1995 to 31 October 1996. (Remember that your year end was 30 April 1996.) The insurance prepayment carried forward from 1 May 1995 was £900.

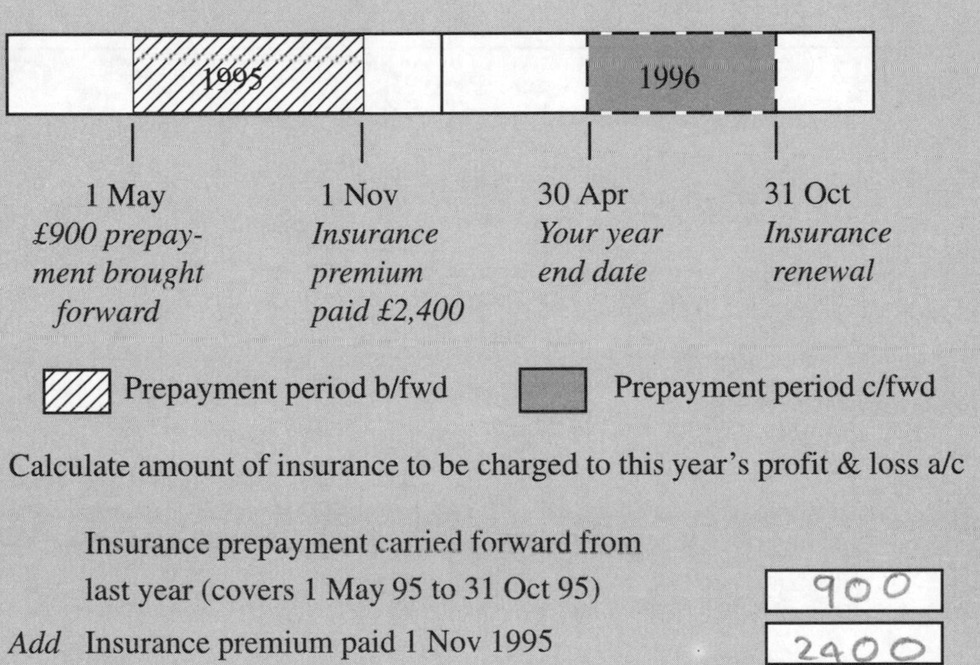

Calculate amount of insurance to be charged to this year's profit & loss a/c

	Insurance prepayment carried forward from last year (covers 1 May 95 to 31 Oct 95)	900
Add	Insurance premium paid 1 Nov 1995	2400
	Total	3300
Less	Insurance prepayment carried forward to new year (covers 1 May 96 to 31 Oct 96)	1200
	Insurance cost for year	2100

Check your answer with the model on page 176. Enter the figure for insurance on the profit and loss account on page 56.

Exercise 4 Accruals

The last electricity bill that you paid was for £600 – this covered the quarter from 1 December 1995 to 28 February 1996. Total payments for electricity this year came to £2,000. There was an accrual for £100 carried over from last year.

ELECTRIC...
1st DEC '95
TO
28 FEB '96
£600

1995 1996

1 May — *Last year's £100 accrual b/fwd*
1 Dec
28 Feb — *Electricity paid £600*
30 Apr — *Your year end date*

Last year's accrual b/fwd

Current year's accrual period (2 months)

We now need to calculate:

(i) Amount of electricity to be accrued for the y/e 30 April 1996. Assuming that electricity is consumed in similar amounts each month, then a typical quarterly bill will be £600. The last bill took us up to 28 February. Therefore, there must be two months of electricity to be accrued for, totalling:

No of months		Average cost per month		Accrual
	x		=	

(ii) Amount of electricity to be charged to the accounts

	Payments made this year	
less	Accrual carried forward from last year	
	Difference	

Continued

Exercise 4 (Contd)

plus	Accrual for this year (2 months)	
	Amount to be charged to the accounts	

Check your answer with page 177. Enter the figure for electricity used on your profit and loss account on page 56.

Exercise 5 Depreciation

Calculate your depreciation charge from the following information.

You have bought a van costing £3,600. You expect it to last six years with no remaining value at the end of the period.

Depreciation charged to the accounts this year £

Check your answer with page 177.

Make sure that you have entered all the answers on the profit and loss account on page 56 and then work out your profit for the period.

Check your answer with the model on page 177.

Profit and Loss Account – Answer Sheet

Profit and Loss Account for the year ended 30 April 1996

		£	£
	Sales	73700	
Less	**Cost of Sales** (Purchases)	55 200	
	Gross Profit		1 18 500
	Overheads		
	Insurance	2100	
	Electricity	2300	
	Depreciation	600	
	Total Overheads		5000
	Net Profit		23500

If you have any difficulties, see model answers on page 177.

We will now prepare a Balance Sheet.

Here are the figures that you will need for your Balance Sheet.

	£
Freehold property	50000
Stock	6000
Accruals	400
Work in progress	8200
Bank balance	12000
Petty cash balance	100
Prepayments	1200
Van	3000
Purchase creditors	9200
Sales debtors	5000
VAT owed by us	2000
Owners capital brought forward from previous year	70000
Private drawings	9600
Net profit for the year	13500
Owners capital carried forward to next year	73900

First you have to decide in which category the figures fall. Remember the categories are:

- Fixed Assets
- Current Assets
- Current Liabilities
- Owners Capital

If you are not sure where they go, refer to Chapter 4, The Balance Sheet.

Now fill in the balance sheet on page 58. To help you, we have put in the values for 'total net assets' and 'balance carried forward to next year'. See if you can work out the contents of the boxes.

Check your answer with page 178.

Balance Sheet as at 30 April 1996

	£	£	£
Fixed Assets			
Freehold portery	50,000		
Van	3000		53 000
Current Assets			
Stock	6000		
Bank Balance	12000		
petty cash balance	100		
Prepayments	1200		
Sales Debtor	5000		
Work in progress	8200	32500	
Current Liabilities			
Accurals	400		
Creditor	9200		
VAT Owned	2000	11600	
Net Current Assets			20900
Total Net Assets			73900
Owners Capital			
Balance b/fwd from previous year		70000	
Net progit		13500	
Total		83500	
less drawings		9600	
Balance carried forward to next year			73900

Congratulations!

You have now prepared a set of accounts in the way your accountant would. If you cannot agree your Balance Sheet, don't worry. Have another go or refer to the model answers at the back of this book.

Chapter 6

What Your Annual Accounts Tell You

Annual accounts are a summary of last year's trading events. As they are often produced many months after the accounting year end, they are of little value in the day-to-day management of the business. They are primarily intended for three types of external reader.

The first are people outside the business like banks, suppliers, HP companies etc. These people are potential lenders of money. They want to check that they are likely to get back the money that they lend you.

The second interested reader is the Inland Revenue. The Inland Revenue base their income tax or corporation tax demand on the profit figure shown in the accounts. Unlike most casual readers of accounts, the Inland Revenue have a great deal of expertise in understanding finance. They also have a comprehensive databank of statistical information which helps them to check whether your numbers are believable.

The third interested readers are shareholders of limited liability companies (however, one wonders how many shareholders really understand the accounts they are given).

Published accounts are not very informative. This is because companies show the absolute minimum of information that they are required to produce by law. The lateness of the accounts makes them of even less value. Annual accounts do, however, represent an annual milestone as the business progresses. The production of the accounts could serve as a trigger to review the firm's progress with the accountant, bank or any other financial adviser that you may choose.

Some people go overboard devising accounting ratios which they claim help to interpret annual accounts. In practice, many of these ratios are of limited value. We will limit our analysis of accounts to a couple of basic measures of business success.

Remember, if you want to stay on top of your business, you must use *monthly* management figures. This is because they are produced regularly and focus on the key management controls as they actually happen. This topic is covered in Part 2 of this book.

Here are a few ratios to help decide whether the trading year was a success.

Did we Make a Profit?

For most people, the main reason for being in business is to make a profit. In fact, the Inland Revenue insist that, if your business is to qualify as a bona fide trade, it must be run with a view to making profits. This does not, of course, mean that losses invalidate your business, but the intention to make a profit must still be there.

Profit!

There is no law which says you have to distribute all of your profit every year. Indeed, if you leave some of the profits in the business, this could lead to a bigger business and, hence, bigger profits at the end of the day. If you make losses, your business will get smaller and, if you make big enough losses, you will eventually be forced to stop trading. Profit, therefore, is very important. Here are a few checks on profitability.

- Did you make a bigger net profit this year compared with last year? (Remember to allow for inflation) If not, why not? Will this adverse trend continue or is it just a temporary phenomenon?

- Is there a *history* of growing profits? This will show that you have a successful track record of efficient management.

- Are you making as much *gross profit* as other members in your industry? Figures for smaller firms are not easy to establish. Check Appendix 2 for examples of gross profit margins in various sectors. We will look at the significance of the gross profit margin in more detail later.

Profitability Ratios

We can divide profitability ratios into two broad categories:

- Gross profit margins
- Net profit margins.

These two figures provide you with important information which will help you assess the success of your business.

The annual accounts will show your gross profit and net profit in pounds. It is useful to express these profits as a percentage profit on sales. This way, as sales go up and down, you will still be able to check whether you are maintaining the same relative profitability.

Gross Profit Margin

We know that the gross profit is the profit left when you subtract the 'cost of sales' from sales, ie:

	Sales
less	Cost of Sales
	Gross Profit

The gross profit % is calculated as follows.

$$\text{Gross Profit \%} = \frac{\text{Gross Profit x 100}}{\text{Sales}}$$

Here is an example of a gross profit % calculation.

Let's say that the total sales for the year were £50,000 and the gross profit as shown in the accounts is £25,000. The calculation would be as follows:

$$\text{Gross profit \%} = \frac{25000 \text{ x } 100}{50000} = 50\%$$

This figure is important because it gives you an indication of whether:

- prices are at the right level
- you are paying too much for your supplies
- your direct expenses are too high
- you are paying too much for direct labour.

We will see later that the Inland Revenue use the gross profit margin as a yardstick against which to judge your business against other similar businesses. If your gross margin is different to the norm, you could be asked questions.

Net Profit Margin

Let's look now at the net profit %. Net profit remains after deducting overheads from gross profit. The net profit % is expressed as a percentage of total sales as follows.

$$\text{Net Profit \%} = \frac{\text{Net Profit x 100}}{\text{Sales}}$$

Let's look at an example.

Let's assume that total sales were £50,000 and the total net profit was £10,000. The calculation would be as follows:

$$\frac{10000 \times 100}{50000} = 20\%$$

The net profit helps to monitor the business. If the gross profit % is right but the net profit % is low, then this could indicate excessive overheads in relation to the size of the business.

The Inland Revenue does not tend to look too closely at the net profitability ratio because this ratio incorporates overhead expenses which are unique to that particular business. However, the net profit % is an important indicator of how well your business is performing against similar businesses in the locality.

Let's look at an example.

Example

John and Jean run a toyshop. Their trading and profit and loss account for 1995 and 1996 is set out below. Use these figures to complete Exercises 6 and 7 following.

John and Jean
Trading and Profit & Loss Account for the Year ended 30 April 1996

	1996		1995	
	£	£	£	£
Sales		303407		220519
Cost of Sales	256317		173884	
		256317		173884
Gross Profit		47090		46635
Overheads				
Rates and water	1723		1525	
Light and heat	530		557	
Wages	9119		8594	
Use of home as office	250		250	
Printing & postage	2433		2549	
Phone/communication	2549		2136	
Insurance	542		496	
Motor expenses	5171		3357	
HP charges	----		612	
Bank charges/interest	530		1171	
Bank loan interest	4801		6593	
Accountancy	1050		980	
Repairs & renewals	206		49	
Sundry expenses	953		1237	
Bad debts	10283		722	
Depreciation	1728		2254	
		41868		33082
Net profit for the year		5222		13553

Exercise 6

Work out the *gross* profit % for 1996 and 1995 using the spaces below.

		1996		1995
Turnover	£		£	
Gross profit	£		£	
Gross profit %	%		%	

What conclusions can you draw from 1996 based on the above figures? List any factors which you think may have contributed to the fall in the gross profitability ratio?

Compare your conclusions with those given on page 179.

Exercise 7

Work out the *net* profit % for each year and enter them below.

		1996		1995
Turnover	£		£	
Net profit	£		£	
Net profit %	%		%	

Why do you think the net profit % declined?

Compare your conclusions with those given on page 179.

Chapter 7

The External Accountant's Job

Most businesses employ an external firm of accountants to conduct an audit, prepare the annual accounts and negotiate the tax payable with the Inland Revenue. Although much of this work could be done 'in-house', the specialised nature of the job, coupled with the fact that it is only done once a year, means it is usually more cost effective to employ professional accountants.

The service provided by your accountants will depend upon:

- the amount of help that you need
- the amount of help you can afford
- your style of trading (a company will require more of your accountant's time than a sole trader)
- the size of your business.

Because the help required depends upon the type of business, the following notes relate to:

- very small businesses
- sole traders and partnerships
- limited liability companies
- PLCs.

Very Small Businesses

Small businesses with a turnover below £15,000 normally don't need (nor can they afford) complicated accounts. The Inland Revenue recognise this and permit these businesses to submit considerably simplified accounts known as 'three line accounts'. These businesses are generally sole traders. There is no reason why the proprietor cannot settle his or her tax without recourse to an accountant. The 'three line accounts' comprise:

	Total Sales
less	Total Expenditure
equals	Net Profit

There is no need to identify separate items of income or expenditure. Expenditure can be deducted from income to arrive at the net profit. If you submit 'three line accounts' to the Inland Revenue, you should still keep detailed records. This is because the Revenue may subsequently ask you to provide these details to support your accounts.

Sole Traders and Partnerships

Sole trader and partnership accounts are less strictly regulated by legislation than company accounts. For example, there is no requirement for an annual audit unless the business is regulated as a professional body, like solicitors. The accounts of sole traders and partnerships are not available to the public (as are company accounts). If confidentiality is important to you, this could be one of the factors to be taken into consideration.

There is nothing in law to prevent you from preparing accounts yourself and submitting them to the Inland Revenue for approval for tax purposes. Indeed, many computerised accounting packages produce a profit and loss account and balance sheet for you. However, unless you are particularly well versed in making the kind of adjustments that we looked at in Chapters 3 to 5, you will probably find it more efficient to let the accountant do the work for you.

Limited Liability Companies

Company financial accounts are subject to more controls than sole traders or partnerships. A limited company is required by law to have an external audit conducted by a suitably qualified accountant every year unless the turnover falls below £90,000. Companies with a turnover between £90,000 and £350,000 do not require a full audit. However, the company must produce an accountant's certificate which states that certain checks have been carried out.

All company accounts must be submitted to Companies House. They are available for inspection by the public. This is done so that lenders, creditors and investors can get an indication of the company's health. Any outside party can pay a fee and inspect your company's accounts if they want to. Although the contents of company accounts are tightly prescribed by law, they do not tend to be very revealing. This is because the reporting categories are so broad that you can extract little of commercial value from them.

PLCs

PLCs have even more legislation to comply with than normal limited companies. Since March 1992, they have had to include a cash flow statement in their annual financial reports as well as the more traditional profit and loss account and balance sheet. (This requirement can extend to 'normal' companies if they engage in special activities like banking, insurance and financial services.)

The Accountant's Job

In general, your external accountant/auditor will:

- Prepare your annual accounts. Usually a draft set of accounts is prepared first, the accountant then discusses these with you.
- Following these discussions, the accountant will make any necessary adjustments. He will then prepare the annual accounts for submission to the Inland Revenue.
- Your accountant should review the annual accounts with you and discuss your business performance. This will highlight current problems and help you to plan ahead.
- Your accountant should look for inconsistencies between the current year and previous years. He should discuss the reasons thoroughly with you. This could be important when dealing with the Inland Revenue at a later stage.
- Your accountant will prepare a tax computation (see later) and advise you of any future tax liabilities. This will help you to make provision for payment.
- Your accountant will submit your final accounts with your tax computation to the Tax Inspector together with any explanatory comments that he may feel necessary.

Of course, there are any number of additional tasks your firm of accountants can perform. These include preparation of cash flow forecasts, credit control, tax planning and preparation of personal tax returns. The extent of the service required will depend on the size and amount of financial expertise available within the business. Often your accountant's advice will save more money than the advice actually costs.

Let's see how your accountant uses the information gathered above when submitting your accounts to the Inland Revenue.

Your Accountant's Dealings With the Inland Revenue

All business accounts are submitted to the Inland Revenue where they are 'screened' by an experienced Inspector. The Inspector examines the accounts to check for irregularities or inconsistencies. These could indicate that they are not a true reflection of the business' trading activities. The majority of accounts submitted are readily agreed by the Inspector.

Tax legislation gives the Inspector far reaching powers. If the Inspector is not satisfied with the accounts, he or she may ask many detailed questions about the business. This will continue until the Inspector is satisfied that the figures are accurate. If the figures *are* accurate, there will be no problem. If the figures *aren't* accurate, the business can incur a penalty of up to 100% of the additional tax plus interest. Indeed, if an Inspector finds a significant error, he has the right to assume this error has been made for the previous six years (and, in exceptional circumstances, for further years also). Unless the business can disprove this, it will be charged tax, interest and penalties accordingly.

Whether the accounts are accurate or not, the business will incur additional accountancy charges if your accountant has to spend time explaining inconsistencies or unusual trends to the Inspector. Remember that the Inspector of Taxes does not have a detailed knowledge of your business. He can only see the figures provided in this year's accounts, together with the comparative figures for the previous year. It is essential, therefore, that your accountant explains the reasons for inconsistencies or unusual trends when submitting your accounts. This will avoid unnecessary questions being raised. There are often good reasons for variations in trading performance but the Inspector will not know these reasons unless he is told. A good accountant will try to get it right first time. The vast majority of accounts are agreed straight away.

Let's examine some of the areas the Inspector will look at when he screens your accounts.

What does the Inspector look for?

Gross Profit Margin

In Chapter 6 we worked out how to calculate the gross profit margin. The Inspector at each tax district has at his/her disposal a 'district profile'. This document lists the gross profit margins of all businesses registered within that tax district. It is constantly updated. This profile is sub divided into types of business. The Inspector will have a very good idea how businesses like yours are currently performing. He will use this as a yardstick against which to judge your gross profit margin.

Your accountant should also have a good idea of what sort of gross margin your business should achieve. If this is significantly at variance with others (for better or worse) then your accountant should discuss this with you and convey the reasons to the Inspector when submitting the accounts.

The Inspector will compare your gross profit margin with that of the previous year. If there is a significant difference, he will ask why. If there are valid reasons, explain them when the accounts are submitted.

Turnover

Although the gross profit margin is a good indicator of your business performance, the Inspector will also look at your turnover. He will compare it with similar businesses in the locality. This is particularly significant for cash businesses, where it is easy to fiddle. Don't be tempted. The Inspector will also compare your turnover with previous years. If there is an unusual pattern (either positive or negative), tell the Inspector via your accountant.

Drawings/Directors' Remuneration

For smaller businesses, the Inspector will check that the amount of money withdrawn from the business by the owners/directors is sufficient to maintain their living standards. If an owner's wages or drawings vary from one year to the next, he should tell the Inspector (via the accountant) why. These variations may well be due to personal circumstances.

Capital Introduced

If the owners inject capital into the business, they should tell the Inspector where the money came from, as he will invariably want to know. An Inspector will need to satisfy himself that the capital introduced has not come from another undeclared source of income or from understated profits. Tell the Inspector, via your accountant, where the money came from at the outset.

Variations in Overheads

Be careful if business overheads vary significantly from year to year. This could raise questions in the mind of the Inspector. If the variations are caused by legitimate expansions or contractions of business activity, explain the reasons for the changes. If necessary, provide a cost schedule to demonstrate why the changes occurred.

Private Use and Non Allowable Items

Sole traders and partnerships often show items in the profit and loss account which have an element of private use. Examples include goods taken for own use, private motoring expenses, parking fines, use of home telephone, entertaining expenses etc. These items are non allowable for taxation purposes. If there are both business and private elements of expenditure, agree with your accountant what percentage is private. The accountant will either reduce the expense in the profit and loss account or add back the private element within the taxation computation (this is explained later).

Sole traders and partnerships should be as accurate as possible when advising their accountants of private use items. Where there is dual use, it is important to separate the private element. It is not worth getting caught out for small gain. If the private use element varies significantly in any year, advise the accountant. He will use the same percentage for private use as the previous year unless he is advised differently.

A Note on Accountants' Fees

Unless the business agrees a set fee with the accountant, fees will be based on an hourly basis. To keep bills to a minimum, the business's own staff should do as much accounting work as they can. The earlier sections of this book explain the information that the accountant needs to gather. It also explains the adjustments he has to make. If you have the information available for him on time, you will save both time and money.

Exercise 8 Taxation

Let us now consider an example. Have a look at the profit and loss account and capital account of Jack Jones the Butcher for the year ended 30 April 1996 on pages 78 and 79. Note that there are comparative figures for the year ended 30 April 1995. During the year to 30 April 1996, the following events occurred.

- Jack expanded his selling space by obtaining the lease of the premises next door. More customers were attracted to his shop as a result.
- Jack inherited £70,000 from the estate of a long lost aunt.

Continued

Exercise 8 (Contd)

- To cope with the additional demand, Jack took on additional sales staff.
- Jack advertised extensively through his local radio station.
- Jack decided it would be cheaper to transport his own stock from the wholesaler. He previously relied on wholesalers deliveries. Jack sold his old van and purchased a new van to carry the increased number of goods.

Have a go at the following.

1 Calculate the gross profit margin for each year.

2 Are there any comments that you would want to submit with the profit and loss account to the tax inspector?

3 Are there any comments that you would want to submit to the Inspector of Taxes regarding Jack Jones' capital account.

Compare your answers with those shown on pages 180 and 181.

Jack Jones The Butcher
Profit and Loss Account for the Year Ended 30 April 1996

	Y/e 30 Apr 96		Y/e 30 Apr 95	
	£	£	£	£
Sales		98294		51480
Deduct Purchases	51269		35449	
Less Stock at 30.4.96	12293		11269	
		38976		24180
Gross Profit		59318		27300
Other Income				
Building Society interest		2362		2103
Profit on sale of van		1000		-----
		62680		29403
Expenses				
Wages & NIC	5916		1058	
Rates	1629		1153	
Light & heat	859		427	
Print/stationery/advertising	3297		963	
Postage	296		210	
Motor expenses	3298		1034	
Entertaining	440		300	
Telephone	629		524	
Parking fines	96		----	
Insurance	870		430	
Bank charges & interest	318		392	
Accountancy	950		540	
Legal costs	800		----	
Cleaning expenses	464		280	
Depreciation	9500		6820	
Loss on sale of car	-----		500	
		29362		14631
Net Profit		33318		14772

Jack Jones The Butcher
Capital Account for the Year Ended 30 April 1996

	Y/ended 30 Apr 96	Y/ended 30 Apr 95
	£	£
Opening Capital	18969	33499
Capital Introduced	30000	-
Profit for Year	33318	14772
	82287	48271
Less Drawings	9873	29302
Balance Carried Forward	72414	18969

Working Out the Tax

Your accountant will prepare a taxation computation for the Inland Revenue. Remember, you rarely pay tax on the *unadjusted* profit shown in the profit and loss account. As we have seen in many smaller businesses, the profit and loss account often includes items which are non allowable (or only partly allowable) because of the private use element. For taxation purposes, we must therefore 'add back' all these non allowable expenses. This will give us our true taxable net profit.

We have seen that the entire purchase price of a fixed asset cannot be charged against the profit in the year of acquisition. Instead, the cost is spread over a number of years in the form of depreciation. The taxman, however, does not recognise depreciation as a business expense. So any deductions from your accounts in the form of depreciation have to be added back to the profit for taxation purposes. However, the Inland Revenue *do* allow an alternative form of relief for capital purchases called 'capital allowances'. Capital allowances are explained in the 'Taxation' book. Suffice to say for the present, capital allowances work in a similar way to reducing balance depreciation. The annual level of capital allowances is decided by tax legislation. Capital allowances are set against the tax adjusted profit (as shown in the next example).

If there are any items of expenditure in the profit and loss account which relate to the disposal of capital assets, these too must be adjusted for in the tax computation. Capital assets can be disposed of for more or less than their depreciated value. Where this happens, there will be a profit or loss on sale. A profit on sale would be treated as income in the profit and loss account. A loss on the sale would be treated as an expense in the profit and loss account.

Sometimes the profit and loss account includes items which are not the result of trading activity. These items have to be deducted to arrive at the tax adjusted profit. For example, it is quite common to see bank or building society interest on deposits included in a sole trader's profit and loss account as income. Interest needs to be *deducted* because it is not part of *trading* income. Interest is treated as investment income. It is either taxed on the individual or, in the case of the company, charged separately from trading profit for corporation tax purposes.

When all adjustments have been made by adding back or deducting items, we arrive at the 'tax adjusted profit' (see example following). Tax is charged on this amount after deducting capital allowances.

Example

We will now calculate the 'tax adjusted profit' using the profit and loss account for Jack Jones The Butcher on page 88. The following information will help.

- Inland Revenue has agreed that 20% of Jack's motor expenses are private
- Inland Revenue has agreed that 30% of Jack's telephone expenses are private
- The legal costs shown in the profit and loss account relate to the acquisition of the new lease.

Jack Jones The Butcher
Tax Computation for the Year ended 30 April 1996

	£	£
Net profit per accounts for year		33318
Add back:		
Depreciation	9500	
Motor expenses (20%)	660	
Entertaining	440	
Telephone (30%)	189	
Parking fines	96	
Legal costs	800	11685
		45003
Deduct:		
Building Society interest	2362	
Profit on sale of van	1000	3362
Tax Adjusted Profit*		41641

*Note: Capital allowances are deducted from this Tax Adjusted Profit. The balance is then taxed at the appropriate rates.

You can see that the 'tax adjusted profit' figure is very different to the net profit shown in the profit and loss account.

This is because we have added back to net profit:

- any items which are non allowable, and
- the non allowable element of expenses which are only partially allowable.

Remember to deduct from the net profit any income which is not directly associated with trading.

Now have a go at preparing a tax computation for Jack Jones The Butcher. Use the figures provided for the year ended 30 April 1995 on page 78. Assume that the private use element for motor expenses and telephone expenses remain the same at 20% and 30% respectively. Compare your answers with those shown on page 182.

Exercise 9

Jack Jones The Butcher
Tax Computation for the Year ended 30 April 1995

	£	£
Net profit per accounts for year		
Add back:		
Total Additions		
Deduct:		
Total Deductions		
Adjusted Profit for Taxation Purposes		

Part 2 – Management Accounts

Chapter 8

About Budgets

So far, we have looked at annual acounts. We have said that annual accounts are primarily for the benefit of people outside of the business, like shareholders, the taxman, banks, HP companies, creditors etc. Annual accounts are important but they are only a small part of the accounting scene.

The vast bulk of the day-to-day accounting focuses on the internal needs of the business. These are the management accounts. Management accounts keep management informed of day-to-day changes in things like sales, wages, materials costs, overheads etc. Management accounts can be presented in any format which helps understand the business. Over time, however, the following documents have shown themselves to be particularly valuable.

- The Budget
- The Cash Flow Forecast
- Key Management Reports.

This part of the book examines these documents starting with budgets.

How Budgets Work

Budgeting is the process whereby managers are set targets which they have to achieve in the coming year. In essence, budgeting involves

- formulating a plan
- delegating responsibility for part of the plan to an individual
- monitoring progress on a regular basis.

Let's have a more detailed look at the steps involved in budgeting.

1 Delegate Responsibility

Decide who is responsible for what. Then delegate as much responsibility as possible.

Delegation involves:

- making a single person responsible
- training that person to do their job properly
- supervising the person, also providing help and guidance.

The most powerful form of delegation is to give an employee all the tools to do the job. This includes control over the money reserved for that activity. This makes the employee a *budget holder*.

2 Plan the Master Budget

Senior management sets broad targets for the coming year (covering items such as sales, costs, profit). Everyone needs to know what these broad targets are. These broad targets are contained in the master budget.

The best time to plan the budget for the new year is the final month of your old year. How do you do that? First review the current year:

- has the year been successful?
- has the cash flow been good or bad?
- have there been any major problems which have affected profits?

Taking into account the above factors, start to prepare a draft cash budget and a draft profit budget.

Remember:

- you will need to allow for inflation
- do you need to spend money on new equipment?
- will you be planning to expand?

Taking these points into consideration, you can then amend your budgets again. Budget holders need to be involved even at this early stage. You need to talk to staff and find out their views.

3 Break the Master Budget down into Mini Budgets

A mini budget is the responsibility of one person. Check that each mini budget is feasible within itself and doesn't conflict with the others. Budgets are all about *commitment*. People feel more committed to targets which they have worked out for themselves. After all who knows more about the budget holder's area of responsibility - the boss or the budget holder himself?

Each mini budget needs to be reviewed by senior management because:

- each mini budget needs to relate to the master budget.
- senior management will contribute to the debate based on their longer experience.
- senior management can act as a sounding board. Even if unable to contribute to the detail, they may be able to help budget holders clarify the thinking on their area of responsibility.

– senior management can look out for the 'optimist' and the 'pessimist'. The optimist plans for the best case, which he is unlikely to achieve in practice. The pessimist 'pads' his budget. This will give the budget holder an easy ride over the next 12 months but it won't do much for the business.

Each mini budget should make sense in the light of past performance. It should be challenging but achievable.

4 Coordinate the Mini Budgets

Collect together all of the mini budgets to ensure that they fit together. Check that each mini budget is feasible in the light of the overall plan.

Sometimes a budget holder may decide that he or she cannot achieve their part of the overall plan. This is valuable information since it addresses the problem whilst there is still time to do something about it. It is much easier to handle problems in the planning stage rather than firefight the problem as it actually happens.

Now is the time to check whether the mini budgets 'stack up' against the master budgets. For example:

- Do the combined mini budgets leave sufficient profit in the master budget?
- Are there any bottlenecks? There may be a bottleneck in one area which could restrict the performance of the whole business. Now is the time to address the problem.

In the worst case, it might be necessary to have a whole series of planning revisions before everything fits into place. It is much easier to do this at the planning stage rather than wait until the problems surface later on.

5 Comparing Budgets to Actual

Let's assume that you are now into your new accounting year. You have established your master budget and your budget holders have their targets.

The next step is to hold regular meetings to check how the actual performance compares to the budgeted performance of the business. Make sure that everyone is aware of the deadlines and dates of the review meetings.

Budget review meetings can be weekly or monthly. Most people have their meetings monthly because many accountancy procedures are based on a monthly cycle (like monthly salaries, statements and purchase payments etc). Preparing for 12 monthly meetings places a much lower burden on accounting staff than preparing for 52 weekly meetings.

Budget meetings provide a forum to raise issues which might otherwise be missed. Sometimes it is hard to find time to discuss details in a business where everyone seems to be permanently busy!

If monthly reviews are too infrequent but you do not want to move to regular weekly meetings, why not have a couple of 'flash reports' during the month? Flash reports are quick updates produced by the accounts staff containing the latest management information. They do not involve the formality of a review. They do, however, enable budget holders to check whether they are broadly on track.

6 Take Action

Each review meeting will throw up a string of actions which need to be undertaken if the business is to remain on track. It is important to agree these actions and then 'minute' them. That way, there can be no doubt who was responsible for what. Each review meeting should open with a report on the actions undertaken as a result of the last meeting.

7 Budget Revisions

Budget revisions are allowed. However, if they are too frequent, they will destroy the credibility of the plan.

Summary

Sort out what is important:

- ☐ What *can* be controlled?
- ☐ What *needs* to be controlled?

Present it properly:

- ☐ Ensure people know what is required of them
- ☐ Make it meaningful
- ☐ Make budgeting easily understood by everyone.

Relate it to individuals:

- ☐ Individual responsibility
- ☐ Individual accountability.

Inform individuals of the outcome:

- ☐ Relate their efforts to the result
- ☐ They will feel part of the team.

Chapter 9

Cash Flow Forecasting – The Cash Budget

Introduction

Cash flow forecasting and control is one of the most important aspects of management accounting. The cash flow forecast is easy to prepare. All you need is time, patience and a little common sense.

A cash budget is simply a forecast of:

– where you expect your cash to come *from*
– where you expect your cash to go *to*.

You also need to decide *when* money will change hands. Timing can be of the essence as we will see later in this chapter!

A cash flow forecast will benefit your organisation in several important ways. These are:

- It provides a powerful tool to measure the *actual* cash performance of your business against *expectations*.

- It gives you control of a critical resource. If you get your cash wrong, you can be in serious trouble!

- It will highlight the peaks and troughs of cash availability. These are critical areas of business management.

In this chapter, we will explain how to prepare and use the cash flow forecast. So far, we have used the words cash forecast and cash budget almost interchangeably. Strictly speaking, you will begin with a cash flow *forecast*. Once everyone is committed to achieving that forecast, it becomes your cash *budget*. Budgeting is all about commitment!

Why is Cash so Important?

Cash is the lifeblood of the business. Not only is it important to get the *amounts* of cash right, we also need to get the *timing* right. Consider the following simple example.

Example

John buys 500 widgets for £10,000 on 1 January and agrees to pay for these on 1 February. He sells the widgets on 2 January for £15,000 and agrees to be paid on 1 March. In accounting terms, John has made a healthy profit of £5,000 but, in cash flow terms, he is bankrupt! Although John has sold the widgets for a profit, this profit will not be realised until 1 March when he is paid. However, John has agreed to pay £10,000 on 1 February which (unless he has other funds) he cannot pay.

Although this example is oversimplified, it does illustrate a very important principle. It is only possible to trade profitably in the long term if there is sufficient cash in the system to meet short term debts as they become due. Of course, most businesses have dozens of buying and selling transactions occurring at the same time. However, you still need cash management even if each individual transaction is profitable. Neglecting cash can bankrupt an otherwise profitable business.

The Working Capital Cycle

Before looking in detail at how to prepare a cash flow forecast, let's see how cash moves within a business. This movement of cash is best illustrated by the 'working capital cycle' diagram shown overleaf. The illustration shows a chair maker; we have chosen this example because there are a lot of stages involved in this business. All businesses have at least some of the stages shown in the diagram.

The diagram shows how cash moves through a small manufacturing business. We begin our journey with the pile of cash shown at (1). Some of this cash is spent on wages, materials, heat, light, power etc – this produces work-in-progress shown at (2) and finished goods shown at (3). The finished goods are subsequently sold at (4) and, after an interval to allow for credit given, ie 'debtors' (5), the cash is finally returned to the business to be used again in the next pass round the working capital cycle.

As you can see, the working capital cycle drives movements of cash in:

- **Stocks** (including raw material, work-in-progress and finished goods)
- **Debtors** (money owed to you by your customers)
- **Creditors** (money owed by you for goods and services delivered but not yet paid for)

Credit has an important influence on the movement of cash in the working capital cycle. Because of credit (ie the giving and taking of time to pay), there is a time difference between the time a sale is made and the time when the cash appears in the bank account.

If you have to pay your creditors faster than your debtors pay you, you may need to borrow money until payment is received. In many established businesses, a cash surplus will have accumulated over a period of time. This surplus is used to bridge the gap between the time the sale is made and the time the cash actually arrives.

Working Capital Cycle

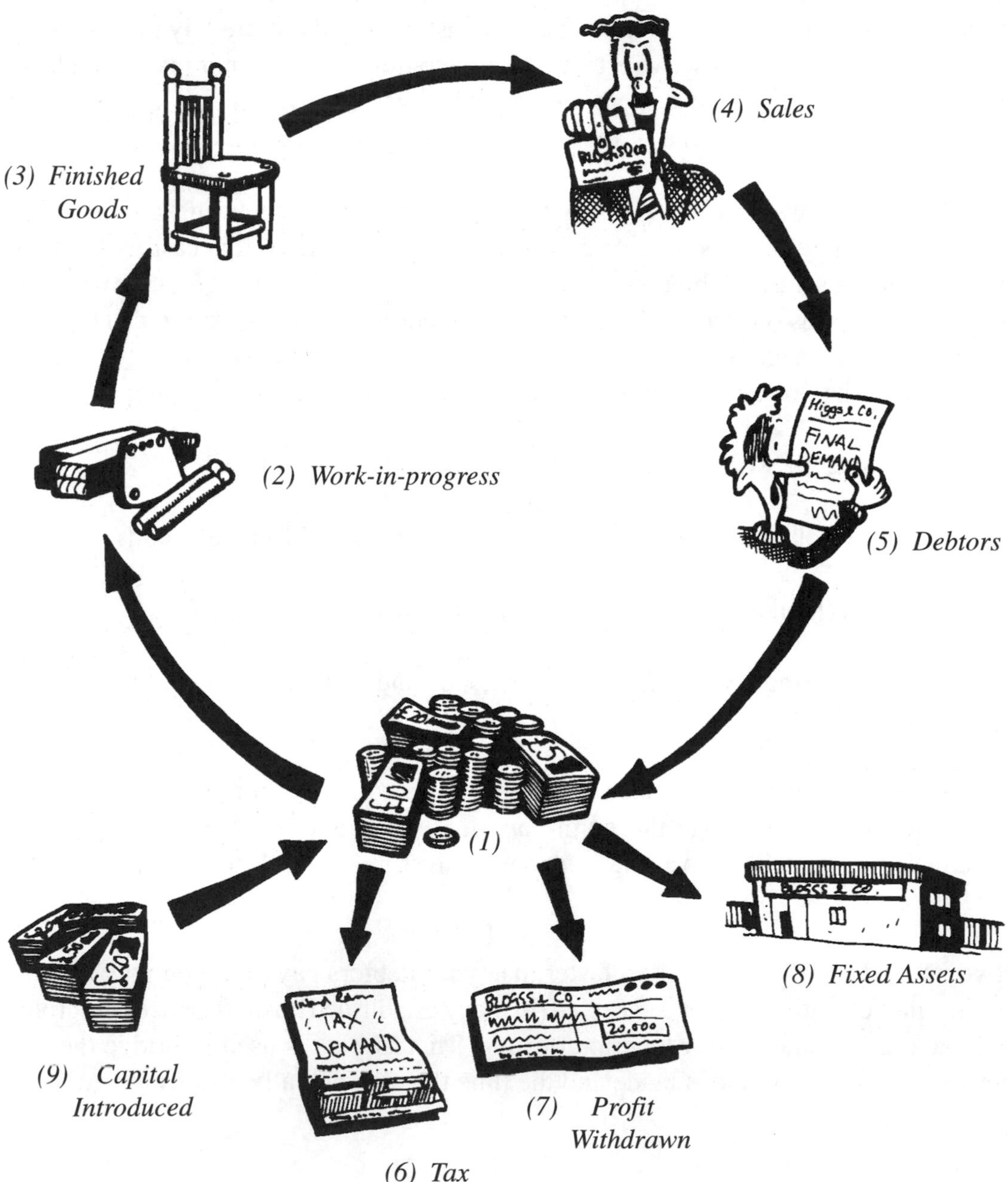

It would be nice if all of our cash could move endlessly round the cycle, growing in value with each pass. There are, however, a number of other cash transactions which can influence the cash pile shown in (1) next page. These include:

Tax — Every business has to pay tax on its profits. This will be either Schedule D or Corporation Tax, depending on whether the business trades as a sole trader, partnership or as a limited company. It will also have to pay employer's National Insurance contributions based on the wages of its employees. This is shown at (6).

Profit Withdrawn — The owners of the business need to be rewarded. If the business is a sole trader or partnership, cash will be withdrawn in the form of 'drawings'. If the business is a company then the directors will be paid wages or salaries. Shareholders may also share in the profits in the form of 'dividends'. This withdrawal of cash is shown at (7).

Equipment Purchases — Periodically our 'fixed assets' (like vans, equipment, office furniture etc) need to be replaced. These items can be purchased in various ways including HP, lease or outright purchase. This is shown at (8).

Introducing Cash — We can top up our cash from outside sources. These sources include bank overdraft, capital introduced by the owners and longer term loans such as mortgages. This is shown at (9).

From the above, we can see that a cash flow forecast will help you to predict the movement of cash through the working capital cycle. Now have a go at Exercise 10.

Exercise 10

Choose a business with which you are familiar, list the activities which could have a significant effect on cash flow. Use the working capital diagram as a source of inspiration.

Check your answer with the suggestions on page 182.

Preparing the Cash Flow Forecast

You control cash using a cash flow forecast. The cash flow forecast is a prediction of how much cash will flow into the business and how much cash will flow out of the business during the same period of time.

In this context, 'cash' includes money paid by cheque, direct debit and credit card payment as well as actual cash itself.

Normally you will prepare your forecast for a year ahead.
This is because:

- a year ahead is about as far as most people can predict with any accuracy.
- a year includes most patterns of seasonality. For example, a tourist hotel would expect high sales in the summer with little or no sales in the winter months.

The cash flow forecast will normally be broken down into months. This enables the trading position to be reviewed on an ongoing basis. Of course, you could elect to review your cash flow weekly but this can generate an enormous workload for the accounts staff.

Your cash flow forecast will typically include most of the following headings:

- Receipts of cash from customers
- Payments for raw materials and stock
- Payments for other expenses
- Drawings and salaries
- Capital expenditure
- Capital or loans introduced into the business
- Loan repayments and interest thereon
- VAT receipts and payments (if you are VAT registered)
- Taxation and national insurance payments.

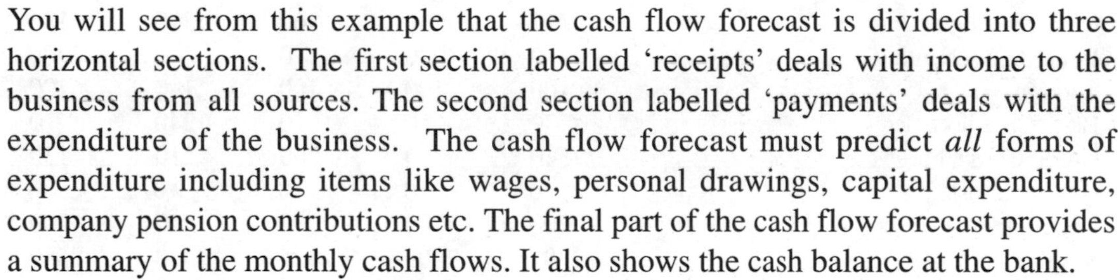

An example of a cash flow forecast (Example 2) is shown on pages 98 and 99.

You will see from this example that the cash flow forecast is divided into three horizontal sections. The first section labelled 'receipts' deals with income to the business from all sources. The second section labelled 'payments' deals with the expenditure of the business. The cash flow forecast must predict *all* forms of expenditure including items like wages, personal drawings, capital expenditure, company pension contributions etc. The final part of the cash flow forecast provides a summary of the monthly cash flows. It also shows the cash balance at the bank.

The example on pages 98 and 99 shows how the cash flow forecast can be used as a powerful budgeting tool for business. It is used to predict the peaks and troughs of cash flowing through the business. It allows management to plan ahead, anticipate future events, and put contingencies in place to allow for them.

Management can spot trends apparent from the forecast and act upon the information immediately – which is the whole purpose of management accounting!

Example 2

Cash Flow Forecast

	MONTH 1	MONTH 2	MONTH 3	MONTH 4	MONTH 5
RECEIPTS					
Cash Sales	25000	20000	22000	27000	25000
Other Income (Rents)	500	500	500	500	500
VAT Output Tax	4375	3500	3850	4725	4375
Capital Introduced	5100	0	0	0	0
TOTAL RECEIPTS (a)	34975	24000	26350	32225	29875
PAYMENTS					
Cash Purchases	12000	11000	11500	13500	12000
Wages & NI	3720	3884	3080	2612	2010
Rates/Water/Rent	2083	2108	1987	1917	1827
Heat/Light/Power	0	0	600	0	0
Repairs/Renewals	0	800	0	0	260
Equipment Hire & Lease	230	120	0	60	0
Insurance	0	0	0	2300	0
Telephone	0	0	525	0	0
Printing/Stationery/Advert	500	400	200	200	200
Motor & Travel	320	200	360	300	180
Legal & Accountancy	0	0	0	0	2000
Sundries	100	100	100	100	100
Bank Charges	130	0	0	240	0
Credit Card Charges	340	380	260	210	130
Bank Interest	0	0	0	0	0
Loan Interest	200	200	200	200	200
VAT Input Tax	2301	2209	2325	2478	2580
VAT Payable (-Refund)	2121	0	0	4890	0
Personal Drawings/Tax	2000	2000	4250	2000	2000
Life & Pensions Contributions	200	200	200	200	200
Capital Exp (Car Purchase)	8000	0	0	0	0
TOTAL PAYMENTS (b)	34245	23601	25587	31207	23687
NET CASH FLOW (d) (a-b)=(d)	730	400	763	1018	6189
OPENING BANK BALANCE (e)	6500	7230	7629	8392	9410
CLOSING BANK BALANCE (d+e)	7230	7629	8392	9410	15599

Example 2

Cash Flow Forecast

MONTH 6	MONTH 7	MONTH 8	MONTH 9	MONTH 10	MONTH 11	MONTH 12	TOTAL
18000	10000	16500	7500	11000	16000	18500	216500
500	500	500	500	500	500	500	6000
3150	1750	2888	1313	1925	2800	3238	37888
0	0	0	0	0	0	0	5100
21650	12250	19888	9313	13425	19300	22238	265488
8380	5880	9630	4550	6760	9840	11390	116430
1624	1324	1874	1090	1348	1732	1922	26220
1769	1724	1806	1689	1727	1785	1813	22235
800	0	0	2400	0	0	1800	5600
0	0	0	0	400	0	0	1460
0	120	0	30	0	0	0	560
0	0	0	0	0	0	0	2300
450	0	0	320	0	0	325	1620
200	200	800	100	100	100	1200	4200
210	140	260	110	120	200	240	2640
0	0	0	0	600	0	0	2600
100	100	100	100	100	100	100	1200
0	150	0	0	95	0	0	615
110	100	145	90	100	120	135	2120
0	0	0	0	0	0	0	0
200	200	200	200	200	200	200	2400
1775	1127	1888	1332	1414	1792	2635	23854
0	5418	0	0	1603	0	0	14032
2000	2000	2000	4625	2000	2000	2000	28875
200	200	200	200	200	200	200	2400
0	0	0	0	0	0	0	8000
17818	18683	18903	16836	16767	18069	23960	269362
3833	-6433	984	-7523	-3342	1231	-1722	-3874
15599	19431	12998	13982	6459	3117	4348	
19431	12998	13982	6459	3117	4348	2626	

Making Cash Flow Projections

The cash flow forecast must be a realistic estimate of future business performance. The accuracy of the forecast will depend on whether the business is established or just starting up.

Existing Businesses

Completing cash flow forecasts for existing businesses is usually a lot easier. Generally you have previous trading results which you can project forward. You will also have experience in managing the business and will therefore be better placed to set the targets which you hope to achieve. Given this information, your forecast is likely to be a more accurate anticipation of business performance.

New Businesses

Preparing a cash flow forecast for a new business can be a difficult task. Often the bank will want to see a cash flow forecast to check whether the business will be viable. In this situation, make sure that the figures are as realistic as possible. The bank manager will not be impressed if the actual trading performance falls drastically below expectations.

If a new owner is purchasing an existing business, he will probably have access to previous trading accounts. These will give a good insight into the income that the business is likely to generate and the types of expenditure likely to occur. It may also be possible to identify other businesses of a similar type in the area. If they are Limited Companies, you can obtain (via Companies House, for a fee) a copy of their latest filed accounts. This may give some clues as to the income and expenditure levels of competitors. Unfortunately, however, the accounts submitted to Companies House are 'abbreviated accounts'. This means that they do not contain a great deal of information. However, they may provide an indication of how well the business should perform.

If you want to pay a fee, you can purchase a personalised report from an agency. These reports give you general information on business performance in your trading sector. In most instances, the report will include details of the catchment area for your business. This may help you to predict likely levels of sales. However, these reports do tend to be expensive.

If you haven't prepared a cash flow forecast before, have a go at Exercise 11 on pages 102 to 106. To make life easier for you, the whole exercise has been printed sideways. If you are familiar with cash flow forecasting, move onto 'tracking the actuals' on pages 108 and 109.

Exercise 11

Use the form on page 106 to complete a cash flow forecast for this business based on the following information. For the purpose of this introductory exercise, we have ignored VAT which will be dealt with later.

Part 1 Receipts

Use the following information to complete the 'Receipts' section of the form attached to page 15.

(i) Capital introduced in month 1 is £2,000

(ii) Cash sales are as follows:

Month	£	Month	£
1	100	7	40
2	150	8	60
3	80	9	100
4	100	10	150
5	150	11	100
6	200	12	70

(iii) Sales invoices were raised in the following months:

Month	£	Month	£
1	2200	7	1200
2	3800	8	1200
3	2600	9	1700
4	1400	10	2600
5	2200	11	1600
6	3600	12	2400

All money from credit sales is received during the ***following month***.

(iv) Sale of assets: £250 is received from the sale of equipment in month 8.

Exercise 11 (contd)

Part 2 Payments

Use the following information to complete the 'Payments' section of the form attached to page 15.

(i) Capital expenditure is made as follows: Month 1 – £600 Month 4 – £900 Month 5 – £2000

(ii) Cash purchases are made as follows:

Month	£	Month	£
1	50	7	-
2	30	8	-
3	-	9	70
4	80	10	70
5	60	11	-
6	-	12	40

(iii) Credit purchases are as follows:

Month	£	Month	£
1	1400	7	1300
2	1400	8	900
3	600	9	900
4	1000	10	700
5	800	11	1000
6	1200	12	900

All credit purchases are paid for in the ***month after*** they are made.

(iii) Other expenditure is as follows:
- – Drawings are taken at £540 per month
- – NI is paid at £20 per month

Exercise 11 (contd)

- Gas and electricity bills are paid:
  - Month 3 – £100
  - Month 6 – £70
  - Month 9 – £50
  - Month 12 – £80
- Telephone bills are paid:
  - Month 2 – £30
  - Month 5 – £50
  - Month 8 – £30
  - Month 11 – £40
- Postage and stationery purchased:
  - Months 2,4,8 & 12 – £20
  - Month 6 – £120
  - Month 10 – £50

(vi) Road tax – £85 is paid in month 2
Car insurance – £135 is paid in month 5
Car servicing bills are paid – £60 in month 4
£80 in month 8

Petrol bills are paid at £35 per month.

(vii) Repairs to equipment are budgeted at £15 per month with additional maintenance of £70 in month 4.
(viii) Business insurances of £450 are paid in month 6.
(ix) Advertising bills are paid at £25 per month with additional amounts of £50 in months 4 and 9.
(x) Professional fees of £200 are paid in month 2.
(xi) Loan interest is paid at £50 per month.

Use the notes on page 105 to help you complete the last three lines of the cash flow forecast.

Part 3 How to Complete Your Cash Flow Forecast

1 Sum the 'Receipts' figures for each month of the year. Enter the totals on the 'Total Receipts' line.

2 Sum your 'Payments' figures for each month of the year. Enter these totals on the 'Total Payments' line.

3 For each month, deduct the 'Total Payments' figure from the 'Total Receipts' figure for that month. Put the difference for each month on the line labelled 'Month's Surplus (Deficit)'. If your 'Payments' exceed your 'Receipts' for any month, show the deficit in brackets (this is the accountant's way of showing negative figures).

4 Now calculate your 'Opening and Closing Balances'. The 'Opening Balance' in Exercise 11 for Month 1 is nil (since this is a new business). The following example shows how to do this. It uses different figures purely for the purpose of illustration. You will need to insert your own answers from Exercise 11.

You will see in the example below the entries for 'Total Receipts', 'Total Payments' and 'Month's Surplus (Deficit)'. In the first month, we had a balance carried forward (from the previous month) of £3,000. We add the Month's 1 total of £1,000 to this to give a 'Closing Balance' of £4,000. This month's 'Closing Balance' becomes next month's 'Opening Balance' so we open Month 2 with an 'Opening Balance' of £4,000. In the case of Month 2, we subtract our 'Deficit' of £750 from the 'Opening Balance' of £4,000 to give us a 'Closing Balance' for Month 2 of £3,250. This, in turn, becomes the 'Opening Balance' for Month 3 and so on.

	Month 1	Month 2	Month 3	Month 4	Total
Total Receipts	6000	1000	4000	2000	13000
Total Payments	5000	1750	3750	2800	13300
Month's Surplus/Deficit	1000	(750)	250	(800)	(300)
Opening Balance	3000	4000	3250	3500	
Closing Balance	4000 ↗	3250 ↗	3500 ↗	2700	

Check your answer with that on page 183.

Cash Flow Exercise

Item	Months												
	1	2	3	4	5	6	7	8	9	10	11	12	Total
Receipts													
Capital Introduced													
Cash Sales													
Credit Sales													
Sale of Assets													
Total Receipts													
Payments													
Capital Expenditure													
Cash Purchases													
Credit Purchases													
Drawings													
NI													
Gas/Electricity													
Telephone													
Postage/Stationery													
Car Tax													
Car Insurance													
Car Servicing													
Petrol													
Repairs/Maintenance													
Business Insurances													
Advertising													
Professional fees													
Loan Interest													
Total Payments													
Month's Surplus (Deficit)													
Opening Balance													
Closing Balance													

A Note on VAT

Businesses which are registered for VAT will find that their cash projections are influenced by Value Added Tax. VAT can have a marked effect on cash flow. Be sure that you build the effects of VAT into your cash flow forecast. HM Customs and Excise do not take kindly to traders who collect VAT and then spend it within their business, leaving them unable to meet their VAT obligations when they become due. This important subject is covered in more detail in Appendix 3.

Will a Computer Help Me?

You can put together a cash flow forecast without a computer. However, if you use a personal computer and a spreadsheet programme, you will save an enormous amount of time and effort. This saving will be particularly noticeable if you run a series of 'what if' calculations. Experimenting with a variety of assumptions gives you a good feel for how variations in sales, purchases, wages etc will affect the business.

Spreadsheet programmes have a further benefit in that the output is neatly laid out in columns. It is easy to insert the 'actual' figures alongside the 'plan' figures once the actuals become available. The results will hopefully impress you, your budget holders and maybe even the bank!

We will explore the way in which computers help with management accounting in more depth in Chapter 13.

Tracking the Actuals

Completing a cash flow forecast is largely a matter of common sense. As the year progresses, you need to check whether the cash flow forecast is in line with the actual trading figures.

You can do this in two ways:

- Most people put an 'actual' column alongside the planned column. This means that each month they record both the 'actual' and the 'forecast' income and expenditure. Turn to pages 116 and 117 – Example 3 where you can see an illustration of this method.

- Some people go further (which is our recommended option). They use a three column cash forecast. The first column shows the 'projected' cash forecast, the second column shows the 'actual' figures and the third column shows the 'variance'. We have calculated the 'variance' as 'actual' minus 'budget' (see example on pages 112 and 113). The variance can be expressed either in pounds or as a percentage variation.

Have a go at the exercise on page 109 which deals with tracking actuals.

Tracking the actuals

Exercise 12 **Tracking the Actuals**

Bill and Ben's Garden Centre

We will use an imaginary business called Bill and Ben's Garden Centre. Look at pages 112 to 115 and you will see that Bill and Ben have completed a cash flow forecast predicting their cash flow for the forthcoming year. The first seven months (May to November) appear on pages 112 and 113. The next five months (December to April) and the 'totals' appear on pages 114 and 115. Notice that the cash flow forecast for each month has been divided into three sections. The first column is the budgeted figure, the second column is for the 'actual' figures and the third column is to show any 'variance'.

Part 1

Notice that no 'actuals' or 'variances' are shown on page 115 for March 1996 or April 1996. The actuals and variances are also missing from the annual totals on the same page. Fill in the missing values for actual and variance for March, April and the totals columns using the information supplied in Table 1 on page 118.

Continued overleaf

Exercise 12 (Contd)
Part 2
Work out the VAT due for the quarter ended January 1996. Remember that the VAT is payable 30 days after the end of the quarter, ie in February 1996. Assume that output VAT on all sales is standard rated, ie at 17½%. Input VAT at standard rate (ie 17½%) has been paid on the following items of expenditure within the cash flow forecast.

- Cash purchases
- Heat, light and power
- Repairs and renewals
- Equipment hire and lease
- Telephone
- Printing, stationery and advertising
- Motor and travel
- Legal and accountancy
- Sundries.

To make things easier, we have totalled the relevant sales and purchases figures for you below. Work out the VAT and check your answers with the worksheet.

	Nov	Dec	Jan	Total
Output VAT				
Sales (excl VAT)	11449	9826	6628	27903
VAT @ 17½%				
Input VAT				
Purchases (excl VAT)	10205	11359	6909	28473
VAT @ 17½%				

VAT Calculation

	Total of Output VAT	
less	Total of Input VAT	
	VAT payable by 29 Feb 1996	

Continued

Exercise 12 (Contd)

Part 3

In December 1995, thieves stole all of the Garden Centre's Christmas trees. These were not insured because they were located in an outdoor sales area.

- Can you spot the effect of the theft on the cash flow of the business? *and*
- Can you see what steps were taken by Bill and Ben to rectify the situation?

Part 4

Briefly comment, in general terms, on the overall cash flow forecast for the year.

Compare your answers with those given on pages 184 to 187.

Exercise 12 – Bill and Ben's Garden Centre

Cash Flow Showing Budget, Actual and Variance Figures May 1995 – July 1995

	MAY			JUNE			JULY		
	BUD	ACT	VAR	BUD	ACT	VAR	BUD	ACT	VAR
RECEIPTS									
Cash Sales	44000	46285	2285	47000	41690	-5310	34000	38245	4245
Other Trading Income	500	500	0	500	500	0	500	500	0
VAT Output Tax	7700	8100	400	8225	7296	-929	5950	6693	743
Capital Introduced	0	0	0	0	0	0	0	0	0
TOTALS (a)	52200	54885	2685	55725	49486	-6239	40450	45438	4988
PAYMENTS									
Cash Purchases	27900	29655	1755	30080	28269	-1811	21100	26422	5322
Wages & NIC	3720	3562	-158	3884	3824	-60	3080	3021	-59
Rates/Water/Rent	2083	2083	0	2108	2232	124	1987	2104	117
Heat/Light/Power	0	0	0	0	0	0	600	960	360
Repairs/Renewals	0	0	0	800	0	-800	0	0	0
Equip/Hire/Lease	230	230	0	120	120	0	0	0	0
Insurance	0	0	0	0	0	0	0	0	0
Telephone	0	0	0	0	0	0	525	724	199
Print/Stat/Advert	500	220	-280	400	329	-71	200	369	169
Motor & Travel	320	482	162	200	333	133	360	269	-91
Legal & Accountancy	0	0	0	0	0	0	0	0	0
Sundries	100	128	28	100	149	49	100	202	102
Bank Charges	130	130	0	0	0	0	0	0	0
Credit Card Charges	340	382	42	380	264	-116	260	302	42
Bank Interest	0	0	0	0	0	0	0	0	0
Loan Interest	200	200	0	200	200	0	200	200	0
VAT Input Tax	5084	5375	291	5548	5110	-438	4005	5066	1061
VAT Payable(-Refund)	2121	2121	0	0	0	0	0	0	0
Drawings/Tax	2000	2000	0	2000	2000	0	4250	4250	0
Life & Pensions Cont	200	200	0	200	200	0	200	200	0
TOTAL PAYMENTS (b)	44928	46768	1840	46020	43030	-2990	36867	44089	7222
Net Cash Flow (a-b) = (d)	7272	8117	845	9705	6456	-3249	3583	1349	-2234
Opening Bank Balance = (e)	1050	1050	0	8322	9167	845	18027	15623	-2405
Closing Bank Balance = (d+e)	8322	9167	845	18027	15623	-2405	21610	16972	-4638

Exercise 12 (Contd) – Bill and Ben's Garden Centre

Cash Flow Showing Budget, Actual and Variance Figures August 1995 – November 1995

AUGUST			SEPTEMBER			OCTOBER			NOVEMBER		
BUD	ACT	VAR	BUD	ACT	VAR	BUD	ACT	VAR	BUD	ACT	VAR
27000	28320	1320	19500	16120	-3380	14000	10233	-3767	10000	11449	1449
500	500	0	500	500	0	500	500	0	500	500	0
4725	4956	231	3413	2821	-592	2450	1791	-659	1750	2004	254
0	0	0	0	0	0	0	0	0	0	0	0
32225	33776	1551	23413	19441	-3972	16950	12524	-4426	12250	13953	1703
16440	17190	750	11950	10320	-1630	8380	7495	-885	5880	6278	398
2612	2826	214	2010	1919	-91	1624	1684	60	1324	1221	-103
1917	1928	11	1827	1627	-200	1769	1616	-153	1724	1549	-175
0	0	0	0	0	0	800	752	-48	0	0	0
0	548	548	260	0	-260	0	0	0	0	3259	3259
0	60	60	0	0	0	0	0	0	120	120	0
2300	2520	220	0	0	0	0	0	0	0	0	0
0	0	0	0	0	0	450	362	-88	0	0	0
200	182	-18	200	262	62	200	149	-51	200	220	20
300	292	-8	180	282	102	210	140	-70	140	189	49
0	0	0	2000	2000	0	0	0	0	0	0	0
100	111	11	100	122	22	100	104	4	100	139	39
240	240	0	0	0	0	0	0	0	150	150	0
210	225	15	130	109	-21	110	102	-8	100	162	62
0	0	0	0	0	0	0	0	0	0	0	0
200	200	0	200	200	0	200	200	0	200	200	0
2982	3217	235	2571	2273	-298	1775	1575	-200	1127	1786	659
7238	6538	-700	0	0	0	0	0	0	3275	2503	-772
2000	2000	0	2000	2000	0	2000	2000	0	2000	2000	0
200	200	0	200	200	0	200	200	0	200	200	0
36939	38277	1338	23628	21314	-2314	17818	16379	-1439	16540	19976	3436
-4714	-4501	213	-215	-1873	-1658	-868	-3855	-2987	-4290	-6023	-1733
21610	16972	-4638	16896	12471	-4425	16681	10598	-6083	15813	6743	-9070
16896	12471	-4425	16681	10598	-6083	15813	6743	-9070	11523	720	-10803

Exercise 12 (Contd) – Bill and Ben's Garden Centre

Cash Flow Showing Budget, Actual and Variance Figures December 1995 – January 1996

	DECEMBER			JANUARY		
	BUD	ACT	VAR	BUD	ACT	VAR
RECEIPTS						
Cash Sales	16500	9826	-6674	7500	6628	-872
Other Trading Income	500	500	0	500	500	0
VAT Output Tax	2888	1720	-1168	1313	1160	-153
Capital Introduced	0	0	0	0	20000	20000
TOTALS (a)	19888	12046	-7842	9313	28288	18975
PAYMENTS						
Cash Purchases	9630	9752	122	4550	4228	-322
Wages & NIC	1874	1942	68	1090	976	-114
Rates/Water/Rent	1806	1602	-204	1689	1436	-253
Heat/Light/Power	0	0	0	2400	1829	-571
Repairs/Renewals	0	0	0	0	0	0
Equip/Hire/Lease	0	0	0	30	30	0
Insurance	0	0	0	0	0	0
Telephone	0	0	0	320	440	120
Print/Stat/Advert	800	1069	269	100	0	-100
Motor & Travel	260	390	130	110	203	93
Legal & Accountancy	0	0	0	0	0	0
Sundries	100	148	48	100	179	79
Bank Charges	0	0	0	0	0	0
Credit Card Charges	145	129	-16	90	112	22
Bank Interest	0	0	0	0	220	220
Loan Interest	200	200	0	200	200	0
VAT Input Tax	1888	1988	100	1332	1209	-123
VAT Payable (-Refund)	0	0	0	0	0	0
Drawings/Tax	2000	2000	0	4625	4625	0
Life & Pensions Cont	200	200	0	200	200	0
TOTAL PAYMENTS (b)	18903	19420	517	16836	15887	-949
Net Cash Flow (a-b)	985	-7374	-8359	-7523	12401	19924
Opening Bank Balance	11523	720	-10803	12508	-6654	-19162
Closing Bank Balance	12508	-6654	-19162	4985	5747	762

Exercise 12 (Contd) – Bill and Ben's Garden Centre

Cash Flow Showing Budget, Actual and Variance Figures February – April 1996

FEBRUARY			MARCH			APRIL			TOTALS		
BUD	ACT	VAR	BUD	ACT	VAR	BUD	ACT	VAR	BUD	ACT	VAR
11000	14380	3380	16000			18500			265000		
500	500	0	500			500			6000		
1925	2517	592	2800			3238			46377		
0	0	0	0			0			0		
13425	17397	3972	19300			22238			317377		
6760	7333	573	9840			11390			163900		
1348	1282	-66	1732			1922			26220		
1727	1529	-198	1785			1813			22235		
0	0	0	0			1800			5600		
400	0	-400	0			0			1460		
0	0	0	0			0			500		
0	0	0	0			0			2300		
0	0	0	0			325			1620		
100	0	-100	100			1200			4200		
120	149	29	200			240			2640		
600	600	0	0			0			2600		
100	124	24	100			100			1200		
95	95	0	0			0			615		
100	172	72	120			135			2120		
0	0	0	0			0			0		
200	200	0	200			200			2400		
1414	1436	22	1792			2635			32153		
1602			0			0			14236		
2000	2000	0	2000			2000			28875		
200	200	0	200			200			2400		
16766	15020	-1746	18069			23960			317274		
-3341	2377	5718	1231			-1722			103		
4985	5747	762	1644			2875			1050		
1644	8124	6480	2875			1153			1153		

Example 3

Cash Flow Forecast Showing Budget and Actual Figures

	MONTH 1		MONTH 2		MONTH 3		MONTH 4		MONTH 5	
	BUDGET	ACTUAL	BUDGET	ACTUAL	BUDGET	ACTUAL	BUDGET	ACTUAL	BUDGET	ACTUAL
RECEIPTS										
Cash Sales	25000	23254	20000	21569	22000	18659	27000	24896	25000	22143
Other Income (Rents)	500	500	500	500	500	500	500	500	500	500
VAT Output Tax	4375	4069	3500	3775	3850	3265	4725	4357	4375	3875
Capital Introduced	5100	5100	0	0	0	0	0	0	0	0
TOTAL RECEIPTS (a)	34975	32923	24000	25844	26350	22424	32225	29753	29875	26518
PAYMENTS										
Cash Purchases	12000	11255	11000	11485	11500	10114	13500	12996	12000	11689
Wages & NI	3720	3659	3884	3458	3080	3256	2612	3153	2010	2115
Rates/Water/Rent	2083	2104	2108	1896	1987	1758	1917	1796	1827	1874
Heat/Light/Power	0	0	0	0	600	754	0	0	0	0
Repairs/Renewals	0	0	800	0	0	0	0	425	260	211
Equipment Hire & Lease	230	0	120	386	0	241	60	0	0	0
Insurance	0	0	0	0	0	0	2300	2145	0	0
Telephone	0	0	0	0	525	654	0	0	0	0
Printing/Stationery/Advert	500	430	400	225	200	154	200	132	200	114
Motor & Travel	320	245	200	188	360	245	300	266	180	154
Legal & Accountancy	0	0	0	0	0	0	0	2856	2000	0
Sundries	100	147	100	122	100	254	100	89	100	174
Bank Charges	130	124	0	0	0	0	240	213	0	0
Credit Card Charges	340	322	380	254	260	189	210	245	130	103
Bank Interest	0	0	0	0	0	0	0	0	0	0
Loan Interest	200	200	200	200	200	200	200	200	200	200
VAT Input Tax	2301	2113	2209	2171	2325	2173	2478	2934	2580	2160
VAT Payable (-Refund)	2121	2121	0	0	0	0	4890	4652	0	0
Personal Drawings/Tax	2000	1800	2000	1800	4250	3896	2000	1800	2000	1800
Life & Pensions Contributions	200	200	200	200	200	200	200	150	200	150
Capital Exp (Car Purchase)	8000	8000	0	0	0	0	0	0	0	0
TOTAL PAYMENTS (b)	34245	32720	23601	22385	25587	24088	31207	34052	23687	20744
NET CASH FLOW (d) (a-b)=(d)	730	203	400	3459	763	-1663	1018	-4299	6189	5774
OPENING BANK BALANCE (e)	6500	6500	7230	6703	7629	10162	8392	8498	9410	4199
CLOSING BANK BALANCE (d+e)	7230	6703	7629	10162	8392	8498	9410	4199	15599	9973

Example 3

Cash Flow Forecast Showing Budget and Actual Figures

MONTH 6		MONTH 7		MONTH 8		MONTH 9		MONTH 10		MONTH 11		MONTH 12		TOTAL	
BUDGET	ACTUAL	BUDGET	ACTUAL	BUDGET	ACTUAL	BUDGET	ACTUAL	BUDGET	ACTUAL	BUDGET	ACTUAL	BUDGET	ACTUAL	BUDGET	ACTUAL
18000	18663	10000	12534	16500	14222	7500	5244	11000	13588	16000	15477	18500	19103	216500	209352
500	500	500	500	500	500	500	500	500	500	500	500	500	500	6000	6000
3150	3266	1750	2193	2888	2489	1313	918	1925	2378	2800	2708	3238	3343	37888	36637
0	0	0	0	0	0	0	0	0	0	0	0	0	0	5100	5100
21650	22429	12250	15227	19888	17211	9313	6662	13425	16466	19300	18685	22238	22946	265488	257089
8380	8665	5880	6877	9630	8865	4550	3899	6760	7863	9840	8642	11390	12674	116430	115024
1624	1569	1324	1254	1874	1956	1090	1458	1348	1366	1732	2436	1922	2568	26220	28248
1769	1625	1724	1489	1806	1752	1689	1675	1727	1856	1785	1654	1813	1689	22235	21168
800	746	0	0	0	0	2400	1742	0	0	0	0	1800	1345	5600	4587
0	0	0	0	0	0	0	0	400	0	0	0	0	0	1460	636
0	234	120	0	0	0	30	253	0	0	0	0	0	0	560	1114
0	0	0	0	0	0	0	0	0	0	0	0	0	0	2300	2145
450	344	0	0	0	0	320	258	0	0	0	0	325	245	1620	1501
200	108	200	122	800	413	100	156	100	145	100	165	1200	689	4200	2853
210	178	140	195	260	243	110	156	120	195	200	145	240	168	2640	2378
0	0	0	452	0	0	0	0	600	0	0	254	0	0	2600	3562
100	56	100	85	100	198	100	143	100	85	100	67	100	95	1200	1515
0	0	150	168	0	0	0	0	95	102	0	0	0	0	615	607
110	98	100	189	145	154	90	104	100	146	120	98	135	175	2120	2077
0	0	0	0	0	0	0	0	0	0	0	0	0	0	0	0
200	200	200	200	200	200	200	200	200	200	200	200	200	200	2400	2400
1775	1808	1127	1353	1888	1701	1332	1156	1414	1450	1792	1623	2635	2663	23854	23305
0	0	5418	4596	0	0	0	0	1603	1390	0	0	0	0	14032	12759
2000	1800	2000	1800	2000	1800	4625	4256	2000	1800	2000	1800	2000	1800	28875	26152
200	150	200	150	200	150	200	150	200	150	200	150	200	150	2400	1950
0	0	0	0	0	0	0	0	0	0	0	0	0	0	8000	8000
17818	17581	18683	18930	18903	17432	16836	15606	16767	16748	18069	17234	23960	24461	269362	261981
3833	4848	-6433	-3703	984	-221	-7523	-8945	-3342	-283	1231	1452	-1722	-1515	-3874	-4893
15599	9973	19431	14821	12998	11119	13982	10898	6459	1953	3117	1671	4348	3122		
19431	14821	12998	11119	13982	10898	6459	1953	3117	1671	4348	3122	2626	1607		

Table 1

Bill and Ben's Garden Centre
Actual Trading Results

(All figures exclude VAT)

	March Actual	April Actual	Totals Actual
RECEIPTS			
Cash Sales	18390	24625	266191
Other Trading Income	500	500	6000
VAT Output Tax	3218	4309	46585
Capital Introduced	0	0	20000
PAYMENTS			
Cash Purchases	11230	14391	172563
Wages & NIC	2004	2239	26500
Rates/Water/Rent	1926	2007	21639
Heat/Light/Power	0	1426	4967
Repairs/Renewals	0	0	3807
Equip/Hire/Lease	0	0	560
Insurance	0	0	2520
Telephone	0	293	1819
Print/Stat/Advert	190	1435	4425
Motor & Travel	269	374	3372
Legal & Accountancy	0	0	2600
Sundries	118	155	1679
Bank Charges	0	0	615
Credit Card Charges	164	122	2245
Bank Interest	0	0	220
Loan Interest	200	200	2400
VAT Input Tax	2066	3163	34264
VAT Payable (-Refund)	0	0	11062
Drawings/Tax	2000	2000	28875
Life & Pensions Cont	200	200	2400

Exercise 13 Preparing a Cash Forecast

If you haven't used a cash flow forecast so far, you may find the following exercise useful. Take a real or imaginary business and compile a list of cash inflows and outflows.

Cash Receipts

List all ***sources*** of cash that you can think of for the business. Think of realistic numbers to put into your cash flow. Don't forget to account for VAT (if registered). The cash flow budget you produce should be a realistic expectation of business performance.

When you have listed everything that you can think of, show your list to other people. See if they can think of any sources of income which you may have missed. It is much easier to get all your headings right first time. This avoids having to recalculate the whole cash flow at a later date. Enter these sources of cash in the 'receipts' section of the blank cash flow form opposite.

Cash Payments

List all the ways you can spend money in the business.

Unfortunately. there always seem to be more ways of spending cash than acquiring it! You are even more likely to have forgotten some form of spending category. Ask if anyone else can think of any items you may have missed. Try to group similar types of expenditure together. This will help you to find items easily when you come to review the figures later.

Cash Flow Forecast

	BUD	ACT	VAR	BUD	ACT	VAR	BUD	ACT	VAR
RECEIPTS									
TOTAL RECEIPTS									
PAYMENTS									
TOTAL PAYMENTS									
Month's Surplus (Deficit) Opening Balance Closing Balance									

Cash Flow Forecast

BUD	ACT	VAR	BUD	ACT	VAR	BUD	ACT	VAR	BUD	ACT	VAR

Cash Flow Forecast

	BUD	ACT	VAR	BUD	ACT	VAR
RECEIPTS						
TOTAL RECEIPTS						
PAYMENTS						
TOTAL PAYMENTS						
Month's Surplus (Deficit) Opening Balance Closing Balance						

Cash Flow Forecast

									TOTALS		
BUD	ACT	VAR	BUD	ACT	VAR	BUD	ACT	VAR	BUD	ACT	VAR

Chapter 10

Managing Cash

Inevitably, there will be times when your cash flow is under pressure. The following notes may help you manage your cash flow better.

Managing Cash In

Most of your 'cash in' will come from sales. If you have the choice between selling on cash or on credit, sell as much as possible for 'cash' because:

- you don't have to wait until the customer eventually pays you.
- chasing your customer for debt costs money and ties up your administration effort.
- giving customers credit is the equivalent of giving them an interest free unsecured loan for as long as they can get away with it. In order to give *them* an interest free loan, you may be running up a bigger bank overdraft yourself. How about offering your customers a discount for cash with order?

Sadly, many customers now regard credit as the norm. You may have no alternative but to sell on credit.

Credit transactions work against the seller. We show below how many steps could be involved between the time you receive an order and the time you get paid.

Steps in Collecting your Cash from Credit Sales

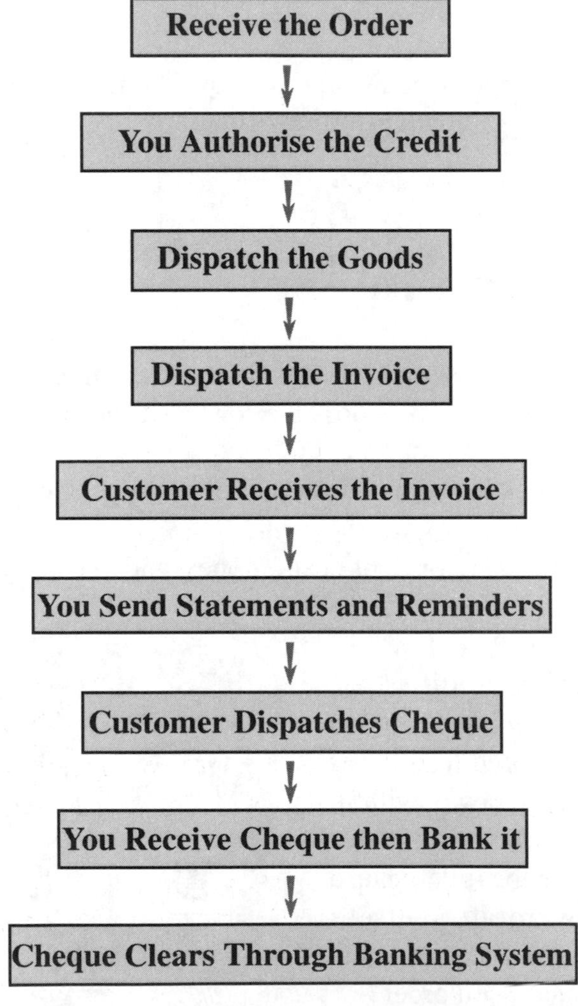

Theoretically, you should receive your cheque within the payment terms stated on the invoice (which is usually 30 days after dispatching the invoice). In practice, the bulk of your cheques will probably arrive between 60 and 90 days after the date you delivered the goods.

Smarten up your cash collection process as follows.

- Only supply goods to customers who are likely to pay. A small number of customers will order goods for which they are unwilling (or unable) to pay. Avoid bad customers by asking for credit references. Get bank references, where appropriate, and only extend large amounts of credit to businesses with a good payment history.
- Send the invoice at the same time as you send the goods. If you perform a service, invoice as soon as you have finished the work. Don't wait until the end of the month to invoice your customers.
- Some customers use a badly drafted invoice as an excuse to delay payment. Don't allow customers to delay payment by querying your invoices. Make sure that your invoices are clear and comprehensive. Quote the customer's order number, where appropriate.
- Send regular statements. If the customer doesn't pay on the due date, phone and politely ask if there is a problem with the goods (or service) or the invoice. If there is a problem, rectify the situation immediately. If not, ask politely why the customer hasn't paid. Also ask when he or she anticipates paying – this could seriously influence your cash flow.
- Continue to chase customers by letter and phone until they pay their bill. Phone calls to the same individual are probably more effective than letters. A visit to their business premises to collect payment often works. Remember, however, that it is illegal to harass your customers.
- Bank the cheque as soon as you receive it. Remember the cash stays in your customer's bank account until it has passed through the banking system. With larger or doubtful cheques, you can get a special quick clearance through the banking system (for a fee).
- Have you considered a prompt payment discount? This may induce your customers to pay early. Unfortunately, some customers take the discount even when they pay late. In this instance, you have to decide whether the loss of customer goodwill is worth the argument over the discount. Only you can tell.

- Make sure that you have a debt collection system in operation. Ensure action takes place at predetermined trigger points. Don't wait until someone feels like collecting debt. Debt collection is one of the worst jobs in the world. You can always find a reason to put it off till tomorrow – don't!

Managing Cash Out

Although you pay cash for some items, you will receive credit from most of your suppliers.

Most suppliers' invoices demand payment in 30 days. However, you may be able to negotiate a longer credit term with your major suppliers because they value your custom. Don't go over the top on late payment, you could find yourself blacklisted so that:

- they monitor your account closely
- you are put on 'cash with order'
- the supplier refuses to deal with you altogether
- you get such a bad name in the industry that *everyone* treats you with suspicion.

You may get a better deal by paying promptly and requesting an extra discount.

Dealing With a Cash Surplus or Deficit

If you are fortunate enough to accumulate cash in hand, don't leave it in your business current account because it will earn little or no interest.

At the very least, open up some form of business deposit account at the bank. Transfer your surplus there. You may find that some building societies offer better rates of interest than your bank. If you have regular, large surpluses, consider talking to your bank, accountant or other financial adviser since there are a variety of short term investments which may generate a better return still.

If you find that you have a temporary cash shortfall, you may need to ask for a bank overdraft. Banks don't respond favourably to sudden demands for instant credit. The best way to get an overdraft is to:

- give the bank copies of your budgets as they are produced so they are informed in advance of your financial position.
- give them plenty of time to react to your request for an overdraft.
- do your homework *prior* to the interview. Take along all supporting paperwork which you may need to convince the bank. If you require an ongoing overdraft, the bank may ask for a business plan showing a cash flow and profit forecast together with details of your future plans for the business.

Surviving a Cash Crisis

Every business seems to experience a temporary cash crisis at least once in its life. Here are some tips on surviving a crisis:

- Radiate confidence, even if you don't feel it. Tell people that you have a temporary cash flow problem – everyone will get paid but there will be a delay.

- Talk to people. If you are still talking to your suppliers, you may be able to convince them that they should continue your credit. If they give up hope, they could take legal action.
- If you can't pay everybody in full, consider paying *some* of the outstanding balance. This will encourage your suppliers since it shows good intent.
- If the worst comes to the worst, only pay essential suppliers. These are people who could stop your business operating tomorrow.
- Negotiate – everyone will negotiate, even the taxman. You won't get the bill written off but you may get extra time to pay.
- Hang in there – sometimes the pressure seems intolerable but you are probably not the only person who hasn't paid their bill on time. To *their* credit controller, you are just another statistic.
- Cut costs – even when it hurts. Staff may have to go even though they don't deserve it. Often the only way to cut expenditure quickly is to reduce the wages bill. Other cash reductions take too long to take effect. Cut back the business to the level at which it is viable.
- Inject cash from outside sources. This may have to be the owners' own funds. You could consider mortgaging the business property if it is freehold.

Cash Management Checklist

☐ Do you have a cash flow forecast?

☐ Does the forecast look achievable in the light of past experience?

☐ Do you revise the forecast when necessary?

- ☐ Are people who are responsible for achieving the forecast involved in setting the budget?
- ☐ Are people with budget responsibility given comparisons between forecast and actual?
- ☐ Do you set time aside for monthly review meetings?
- ☐ Are invoices raised promptly?
- ☐ Do you have an adequate credit control routine?
- ☐ Can you make more cash sales?
- ☐ Do you take enough credit on purchases?
- ☐ Do you need prompt payment discounts?
- ☐ Does the bank have a copy of your cash flow/profit forecast?
- ☐ Is the accounting system adequate to provide cost and sales 'actuals' on time?
- ☐ Do you have proper authorisations for cash spent?
- ☐ Do you have cash tied up in obsolete stock?
- ☐ Can you charge progress payments on large orders/contracts?
- ☐ Is the overdraft under control?
- ☐ Do you need any help from the outside accountants?

Chapter 11

Planning for Profit – The Trading Budget

Small firms will probably find that they can control their businesses perfectly adequately using a cash flow forecast together with 'actuals' supplied from their analysed cash book. Large businesses, however, will need to go further. They will want a cash budget *and* a profit budget.

Before going any further, let's remind ourselves of the difference between a cash surplus and a profit.

Summary of Differences Between the Cash Flow Statement and the Profit & Loss A/c

	Profit & Loss Account	Cash Flow
Sales	Sale recorded when goods/service accepted	Sale recorded when cash received
Materials	Material costs recorded when used	Material costs recorded when paid for
Assets	Asset costs shown as depreciation	Asset costs shown when bought
Overheads	Overheads apportioned to a period	Overheads recorded when paid for
VAT	Excluded from profit calculation	Treated as a cash inflow/outflow
Period	Profit relates to a period. Need to incorporate accruals/prepayments	Cash flows simply added to opening balance

If these differences are not familiar, you may need to review Chapter 3 again.

Profit is extremely sensitive to changes in cost, prices and volumes as the following exercise demonstrates.

Exercise 14

Consider the following profit & loss account:

	Sales	100
less	Cost of Sales	40
	Gross Profit	60
less	Overheads	30
	Net Profit	30

What would be the effect on profit of:

(i) doubling sales?
(ii) halving sales?

Assume for the moment that:

- 'sales' and 'cost of sales' always move in sympathy with each other, and
- overheads remain constant.

(i) **Double Sales**

	Sales	
less	Cost of Sales	
	Gross Profit	
less	Overheads	
	Net Profit	

(ii) **Halve Sales**

	Sales	
less	Cost of Sales	
	Gross Profit	
less	Overheads	
	Net Profit	

Check your answer with the model given on page 187.
Note the dramatic shift in profitability.

It makes a lot of sense to break profit planning down into two stages. The first stage only goes as far as the gross profit line. This is called the **Trading Budget**, as follows:

Trading Budget

	Sales
less	Cost of Sales
equals	Gross Profit

The second stage produces the net profit. This is called the **Profit and Loss Budget**, as follows:

Profit and Loss Budget

	Gross Profit
less	Overheads
equals	Net Profit

We will look at the trading budget in this chapter and the profit and loss budget in the next chapter.

Preparing the Trading Budget

We will now look at ways of preparing the trading budget. This will form a target to which sales staff and production staff will be committed.

Let's prepare a trading forecast based on our imaginary business partnership, Bill and Ben's Garden Centre. For the purpose of this exercise, the firm's accounting year ends on 30 April each year.

Planning

Ideally, you should have two years accounts available to give you a basis on which to prepare your trading budget. Make sure your latest trading accounts are available as soon as possible after your year end. If you have an external accountant who prepares these for you, ask him to produce draft accounts as quickly as possible. If this is not possible, you should attempt to produce provisional figures yourself from your own records. Adjust these later when your accountant produces your annual accounts.

First you need to set out your headings in line with your annual accounts. You can, however, expand each heading if you require further analysis. For example, you may have four or five departments which generate sales. You may want each department separately analysed. You will probably want to break your total sales figures down to show each department separately.

In our example, Bill and Ben run a Garden Centre. They want to forecast their 'sales' and 'cost of sales' so they can see what gross profit they will achieve for each department. The following layout shows one way of analysing sales by department.

Trading Account for Year ended 30 April 1997

	Dept 1 Plants & Shrubs	**Dept 2** Garden Furniture	**Dept 3** Composts etc	**Dept 4** Fertilisers etc	**Dept 5** Other Sales	**Total**
Sales	100000	25000	30000	60000	50000	265000
Less **Cost of Sales**	70000	12500	17000	40000	25000	164500
Gross Profit	30000	12500	13000	20000	25000	100500

In our example, 'sales' would comprise all items sold, irrespective of whether the sale was made by cash or credit. 'Cost of sales' would comprise the cost of items bought for resale plus the cost of rearing any plants grown by the business for selling on to customers. Cost of sales would also include the wages of staff directly concerned with the growing of plants and selling the goods. Other staff wages would appear in overheads. There may also be some 'expense' associated with cost of sales – this could include items such as cost of carriage inwards. Remember if you are VAT registered, all figures appearing in the trading budget will be net of VAT.

After setting out the accounts for the past two years in such a way as to extract as much information as possible, review the accounts in the light of historic and current experience. Remember to take into account any seasonal variations. In the case of our Garden Centre, you would expect a large turnover in the gardening season. This will tail off some months later.

On the opposite page (Example 4) you will see a Trading Budget for Bill and Ben's Garden Centre. Remember their year end is 30 April. It looks complicated but it isn't! Let's see how the figures were calculated. Have a look at any of the columns labelled 'budget' or 'actual'. Notice how 'sales', 'cost of sales' and 'gross profit' are broken down for each department. Also notice that each value has a percentage figure alongside. Let's take one of these figures as an example. Notice that Dept 1, Plant and Shrubs, sales for the year ended 30 April 1995 amounts to 39%. This is how it was calculated:

$$\frac{\text{Plant \& Shrub sales x 100}}{\text{Total sales}} = \frac{70000 \text{ x } 100}{178000} = 39\%$$

Example 4 – Bill and Ben's Garden Centre

Trading Budget From May 1996 to April 1997

	ACTUAL 1994/95		ACTUAL 1995/96		BUDGET 1996/97		BUDGET BY MONTH MAY	JUN	JUL	AUG	SEP	OCT	NOV	DEC	JAN	FEB	MAR	APR
	£	%	£	%	£	%	£	£	£	£	£	£	£	£	£	£	£	£
SALES																		
Department																		
1 Plant & Shrubs	70000	39	85000	39	100000	38	20000	25000	15000	10000	7500	5000	2500	5000	500	2000	3000	4500
2 Garden Furniture	18000	10	22000	10	25000	9	5000	5000	5000	4000	3000	2000	500	500	0	0	0	0
3 Composts	20000	11	23000	10	30000	11	5000	5000	5000	5000	1000	1000	1000	1000	1000	1000	2000	2000
4 Fertilizers etc	40000	23	50000	23	60000	23	10000	8000	5000	4000	4000	2000	2000	2000	4000	5000	7000	7000
5 Other Sales	30000	17	40000	18	50000	19	4000	4000	4000	4000	4000	4000	4000	8000	2000	3000	4000	5000
TOTAL SALES	178000	100	220000	100	265000	100	44000	47000	34000	27000	19500	14000	10000	16500	7500	11000	16000	18500
COST OF SALES																		
Department																		
1 Plant & Shrubs	50000	71	59500	70	70000	70	14000	17500	10500	7000	5250	3500	1750	3500	350	1400	2100	3150
2 Garden Furniture	9000	50	11000	50	12500	50	2500	2500	2500	2000	1500	1000	250	250	0	0	0	0
3 Composts	11000	55	12500	54	17000	56	2800	2800	2800	2800	560	560	560	560	560	560	1120	1320
4 Fertilizers etc	26000	65	32000	64	40000	66	6600	5280	3300	2640	2640	1320	1320	1320	2640	3300	4620	5020
5 Other Sales	15000	50	20000	50	25000	50	2000	2000	2000	2000	2000	2000	2000	4000	1000	1500	2000	2500
TOTAL COST OF SALES	111000	62	135000	61	164500	62	27900	30080	21100	16440	11950	8380	5880	9630	4550	6760	9840	11990
GROSS PROFIT																		
Department																		
1 Plant & Shrubs	20000	29	25500	30	30000	30	6000	7500	4500	3000	2250	1500	750	1500	150	600	900	1350
2 Garden Furniture	9000	50	11000	50	12500	50	2500	2500	2500	2000	1500	1000	250	250	0	0	0	0
3 Composts	9000	45	10500	46	13000	44	2200	2200	2200	2200	440	440	440	440	440	440	880	680
4 Fertilizers etc	14000	35	18000	36	20000	34	3400	2720	1700	1360	1360	680	680	680	1360	1700	2380	1980
5 Other Sales	15000	50	20000	50	25000	50	2000	2000	2000	2000	2000	2000	2000	4000	1000	1500	2000	2500
TOTAL GROSS PROFIT	67000	38	85000	39	100500	38	16100	16920	12900	10560	7550	5620	4120	6870	2950	4240	6160	6510

Check the percentage profit figures for other departments for sales, cost of sales and gross profit to make sure that you can see how each figure is calculated.

To help you, we have reproduced Example 4 on the page opposite with boxes explaining how each percentage was calculated. These gross profit percentages are very revealing. For example, in the year to 30 April 1996, we can tell that our most profitable departments, in percentage terms, were 'Garden Furniture' and 'Other'. Since these departments are so profitable, we may want to increase sales in these areas. This could be done for example by increasing the amount of floorspace devoted to these products and increasing the number of lines carried or perhaps employing more sales staff.

Suppose we found that the gross profit was falling. This might be because:

- we failed to implement proper price increases
- costs from our suppliers had risen
- we may have suffered theft from our customers or even our own staff
- we could be selling too many low margin products at the expense of our high margin items
- competitors are taking too large a share of our market.

These are all good starting points for an investigation into the cause of the downward trend.

We can use our knowledge of past events, together with our experience, to establish the likely sales and profit levels for the coming year. Before implementing the trading budget, be sure to get as much feedback as possible from staff. If Bill and Ben had a sales manager, it would be his job to ensure that the sales projections were achieved. He would only feel committed to the sales forecast if he had an opportunity to influence that forecast. Similarly, if Bill and Ben employed a buyer, he would be responsible for buying at prices which left the kind of margins projected in the budget for next year. This level of personal commitment from all of the members of staff is critical if targets are to be met.

Example 4 – Bill and Ben's Garden Centre

Trading Budget From May 1996 to April 1997

	ACTUAL 1994/95		ACTUAL 1995/96		BUDGET 1996/97		BUDGET BY MONTH MAY	JUN	JUL	AUG	SEP	OCT	NOV	DEC	JAN	FEB	MAR	APR
	£	%	£	%	£	%	£	£	£	£	£	£	£	£	£	£	£	£
SALES																		
Department																		
1 Plant & Shrubs	70000	39	85000	39	100000	38	20000	25000	[illegible]	[illegible]	[illegible]	[illegible]	[illegible]	[illegible]	[illegible]	[illegible]	[illegible]	4500
2 Garden Furniture	18000	10	22000	10	25000	9	5000	5000	[illegible]	[illegible]	[illegible]	[illegible]	[illegible]	[illegible]	[illegible]	[illegible]	0	0
3 Composts	20000	11	23000	10	30000	11	5000	5000	[illegible]	[illegible]	[illegible]	[illegible]	[illegible]	[illegible]	[illegible]	[illegible]	[illegible]	2000
4 Fertilizers etc	40000	23	50000	23	60000	23	10000	8000	5000	4000	4000	2000	2000	2000	4000	5000	7000	7000
5 Other Sales	30000	17	40000	18	50000	19	4000	4000	[illegible]	[illegible]	[illegible]	[illegible]	[illegible]	[illegible]	[illegible]	[illegible]	[illegible]	5000
TOTAL SALES	178000	100	220000	100	265000	100	44000	47000	[illegible]	[illegible]	[illegible]	[illegible]	[illegible]	[illegible]	[illegible]	[illegible]	[illegible]	18500
COST OF SALES																		
Department																		
1 Plant & Shrubs	50000	71	59500	70	70000	70	14000	17500	[illegible]	[illegible]	[illegible]	[illegible]	[illegible]	[illegible]	[illegible]	[illegible]	[illegible]	3150
2 Garden Furniture	9000	50	11000	50	12500	50	2500	2500	[illegible]	[illegible]	[illegible]	[illegible]	[illegible]	[illegible]	[illegible]	[illegible]	0	0
3 Composts	11000	55	12500	54	17000	56	2800	2800	2800	2800	560	560	560	560	560	560	1120	1320
4 Fertilizers etc	26000	65	32000	64	40000	66	6600	5280	[illegible]	[illegible]	[illegible]	[illegible]	[illegible]	[illegible]	[illegible]	[illegible]	[illegible]	5020
5 Other Sales	15000	50	20000	50	25000	50	2000	2000	[illegible]	[illegible]	[illegible]	[illegible]	[illegible]	[illegible]	[illegible]	[illegible]	[illegible]	2500
TOTAL COST OF SALES	111000	62	135000	61	164500	62	27900	30080	[illegible]	[illegible]	[illegible]	[illegible]	[illegible]	[illegible]	[illegible]	[illegible]	[illegible]	11990
GROSS PROFIT																		
Department																		
1 Plant & Shrubs	20000	29	25500	30	30000	30	6000	7500	[illegible]	[illegible]	[illegible]	[illegible]	[illegible]	[illegible]	[illegible]	[illegible]	[illegible]	1350
2 Garden Furniture	9000	50	11000	50	12500	50	2500	2500	2500	2000	1500	1000	250	250	0	0	0	0
3 Composts	9000	45	10500	46	13000	44	2200	2200	[illegible]	[illegible]	[illegible]	[illegible]	[illegible]	[illegible]	[illegible]	[illegible]	[illegible]	680
4 Fertilizers etc	14000	35	18000	36	20000	34	3400	2720	[illegible]	[illegible]	[illegible]	[illegible]	[illegible]	[illegible]	[illegible]	[illegible]	[illegible]	1980
5 Other Sales	15000	50	20000	50	25000	50	2000	2000	[illegible]	[illegible]	[illegible]	[illegible]	[illegible]	[illegible]	[illegible]	[illegible]	[illegible]	2500
TOTAL GROSS PROFIT	67000	38	85000	39	100500	38	16100	16920	12900	10560	7550	5620	4120	6870	2950	4240	6160	6510

$$\frac{\text{Sales for Dept 1} \times 100}{\text{Total Sales}} = \frac{£100{,}000 \times 100}{£265{,}000} = 38\%$$

Check all department sales percentages add up to 100 per cent!

$$\frac{\text{Cost of Sales for Dept 1} \times 100}{\text{Sales for Dept 1}} = \frac{£70{,}000 \times 100}{£100{,}000} = 70\%$$

$$\frac{\text{Total Cost of Sales} \times 100}{\text{Total Sales}} = \frac{£164{,}500 \times 100}{£265{,}000} = 62\%$$

$$\frac{\text{Gross Profit for Dept 1} \times 100}{\text{Sales for Dept 1}} = \frac{£30{,}000 \times 100}{£100{,}000} = 30\%$$

$$\frac{\text{Total Gross Profit} \times 100}{\text{Total Sales}} = \frac{£100{,}500 \times 100}{£265{,}000} = 38\%$$

Notice that the projected annual budget totals for 1996/1997 in Example 4 have been broken down into months. This will allow us to check whether the plan is on course, allowing for seasonal variations. Of course, we could add monthly 'actual' columns alongside the 'budget' columns to check on progress as the year unfolds. We could also work out percentages to check whether the expected 'percentage sales year to date' had been achieved. The key thing about a budget statement is that it should make sense to the people who actually use the document. There are no 'right' or 'wrong' ways of doing budgets. Show the figures in any way that makes sense.

Here is an exercise for you to try. This has been set out on a smaller scale to make it easier for you to complete. We have only used two departments instead of five. Use the worksheet on page 146.

Exercise 15

Playaway is a business which sells toys and educational supplies. Their year ends on 30 April. Accounts for the years ended 30 April 1995 and 1996 have been entered for you on page 146.

1 Work out the budget for sales, taking into account that anticipated sales will increase by 10% for toys and 30% for education supplies over the figure for 1996. Enter this on your working sheet. Next add together the two department sales and enter this figure in the total sales box. Don't worry about the breakdown by month at this stage.

2 Now work out your percentage of sales for each department (toys and educational) in relation to your total sales. This is calculated as follows:

$$\frac{\text{Department sales} \times 100}{\text{Total sales}} = \text{xx}\ \%$$

Continued

Exercise 15 (Contd)

The two departments added together will equal the total sales and the department percentages will add up to 100%. (You will find of course that the percentages are not consistent with 1996 because educational supplies have increased by 30% over the previous year.) Enter these percentages on your worksheet.

3 Next we will work out the cost of sales for each department. The anticipated cost of sales for toys will be 45% of total toy sales. This year, we have managed to obtain additional discounts from suppliers so the cost of sales for educational supplies will be 60% of total educational sales.

For example, the cost of sales for toys will be calculated as:

$$\frac{\text{Toy sales x 45}}{100} = 32175$$

Enter this on the worksheet.

Work out the cost of sales for the educational department. Enter the costs of sales percentages as given above at 45% for toys and 60% for educational supplies.

We can now work out the total cost of sales by adding together the toys and educational figures. Put this figure in the 'total' box. We now need to work out the total cost of sales percentage compared to total sales. This is done as follows:

$$\frac{\text{Total cost of sales x 100}}{\text{Total sales}} = \frac{58695 \text{ x } 100}{115700} = 51\%$$

Enter this percentage on the worksheet.

Continued overleaf

Exercise 15 (Contd)

4 Now work out your gross profit for each department in £ and %. By way of example, we have shown how we calculated the gross profit in £ and % for 1996 actuals.

	Total £	Total %	Toys £	Toys %	Educational £	Educational %
Sales	99000	100	65000	66	34000	34
less Cost of Sales	56300	56	32500	50	23800	70
Gross Profit	42700	44	32500	50	10200	30

To arrive at the gross profit in pounds, simply deduct the cost of sales from total sales for each department. Put these figures on your worksheet (the table above will help). We now need to enter the percentages in the gross profit section.

To arrive at the gross profit percentage, simply deduct the total cost of sales percentage from the total sales percentage (which is shown in the total box in the above example).

A different calculation applies to the departmental gross profit %. This is as follows.

Toys

$$\frac{\text{Gross profit x 100}}{\text{Sales}}$$

Educational

$$\frac{\text{Gross profit x 100}}{\text{Sales}}$$

5 The next stage analyses 'sales' and 'cost of sales' by month taking into account seasonality.

Seasonal *sales* are as follows:

Continued

Exercise 15 (Contd)

- Toy sales in December represent 40% of the total sales. Therefore 60% of toy sales are sold equally over the remaining 11 months of the year.

- Educational supplies in August represent 30% of the total sales. Therefore 70% of educational supplies are sold equally over the remaining 11 months.

Now you can analyse the *cost of sales* by month as follows:

- Annual cost of sales for toys is £32,175 for the Budget year; sales in December are 40% of this figure. This means that 60% of total costs are incurred equally over the remaining 11 months of the year.

- Educational cost of sales in August represent 30% of total cost of sales. Therefore 70% of educational costs are incurred over the remaining 11 months of the year.

Enter all your cost of sales on the worksheet by month. You can now work out your gross profit each month as follows:

	Sales
less	Cost of Sales
equals	Gross Profit

Enter these figures on your worksheet to include both departmental and overall gross profit figures.

You have now entered all your trading budget on page 146. Check your calculations with the model answers on page 188. Have you got it right? If not, review the figures and establish where you have gone wrong.

The next stage is projecting and analysing the fixed and variable overheads and calculating the projected net profit. We will do this in the next section.

Exercise 16 – Playaway

Trading Budget From May 1996 to April 1997

	ACTUAL 1994/95		ACTUAL 1995/96		ACTUAL 1996/97		BUDGET BY MONTH											
							MAY	JUN	JUL	AUG	SEP	OCT	NOV	DEC	JAN	FEB	MAR	APR
	£	%	£	%	£	%	£	£	£	£	£	£	£	£	£	£	£	£
SALES																		
Department																		
1 Toys	50000	63	65000	66														
2 Educational	30000	37	34000	34														
TOTAL	80000	100	99000	100														
COST OF SALES																		
Department																		
1 Toys	25000	50	32500	50														
2 Educational	21000	70	23800	70														
TOTAL	46000	57	56300	56														
GROSS PROFIT																		
Department																		
1 Toys	25000	50	32500	50														
2 Educational	9000	30	10200	30														
TOTAL	34000	43	42700	44														

Chapter 12

Planning for Profit –
The Profit and Loss Budget

So far we have looked at profit planning as far as the gross profit line is concerned. However we still have other costs to meet. These are called overheads. Overheads include items like rent, rates, depreciation, insurance, office salaries etc. In some businesses, overheads can be very significant indeed. Overheads can be split into two types. These are fixed overheads and variable overheads.

Fixed overheads tend to remain at the same level irrespective of the level of business activity. For example, the local council will not reduce your business rates if you have a bad year. By the same token, they won't increase your business rates if you have a good one! Many overheads are fixed in nature. These include depreciation, insurance, rent, rates, supervisory wages etc. It is helpful to group these expenditures together.

Not all overheads are fixed!

Variable overheads vary in proportion to the amount of sales transacted by the business. For example, with Bill and Ben's Garden Centre, we would expect sales to peak during the summer months. To handle this increase in sales, Bill and Ben could take on casual staff who work on a variety of tasks around the Garden Centre according to the needs of the day. These staff would be laid off as autumn approaches when sales fall to a lower level.

Example 5 – Bill and Ben's Garden Centre

	ACTUAL 1994/95		ACTUAL 1995/96		BUDGET 1996/97		BUDGET BY MONTH MAY	JUNE	JULY	AUGUST	SEPT.	OCT.	NOV.	DEC.	JAN.	FEB.	MARCH	APRIL
	£	%	£	%	£	%	£	£	£	£	£	£	£	£	£	£	£	£
GROSS PROFIT B/FWD	67000	38	85000	39	100500	38	16100	16920	12900	10560	7550	5620	4120	6870	2950	4240	6160	6510
VARIABLE OVERHEADS																		
Casual Staff Wages	13400	7	17000	7	20220	8	3220	3384	2580	2112	1510	1124	824	1374	590	848	1232	1422
Water Charges	2010	2	2550	2	3035	1	483	508	387	317	227	169	124	206	89	127	185	213
TOTAL VARIABLE O/HEADS	15410	9	19550	9	23255	9	3703	3892	2967	2429	1737	1293	948	1580	679	975	1417	1635
FIXED OVERHEADS																		
Rent	12000	7	12000	5	12000	4	1000	1000	1000	1000	1000	1000	1000	1000	1000	1000	1000	1000
Rates	6000	3	6600	3	7200	3	600	600	600	600	600	600	600	600	600	600	600	600
Light and Heat	4800	3	5200	2	5600	2	200	200	200	200	200	400	800	800	800	600	600	600
Salaries	5000	3	5500	3	6000	2	500	500	500	500	500	500	500	500	500	500	500	500
Stationery & advertising	2400	1	3600	2	4200	2	350	350	350	350	350	350	350	350	350	350	350	350
Motor expenses	1560	1	2100	1	2640	1	220	220	220	220	220	220	220	220	220	220	220	220
Telephone	900	1	1200	1	1620	1	135	135	135	135	135	135	135	135	135	135	135	135
Sundries	600	0	900	0	1200	0	100	100	100	100	100	100	100	100	100	100	100	100
TOTAL FIXED OVERHEADS	33260	19	37100	17	40460	15	3105	3105	3105	3105	3105	3305	3705	3705	3705	3505	3505	3505
NET PROFIT	18330	10	28350	13	36785	14	9292	9923	6828	5026	2708	1022	-533	1585	-1434	-240	1238	1370

Responsibility for controlling overheads has to be delegated to a named person. For example, you could delegate:

- sales administration costs to the sales director
- purchase administration costs to the buying director
- fixed overheads to the office manager.

Let's illustrate the profit and loss budget by reference to Bill and Ben's Garden Centre again. Please refer to Example 5 on the opposite page. Notice how we have carried down the gross profit figures from our trading budget. These now appear in the top line of our profit and loss budget. The next section focuses on variable overheads. In this instance, two types of expenditure are included; these are casual staff wages and water consumption. A great deal more water is used during the peak buying season.

Casual Labour

Below variable overheads, we have listed fixed overheads. Notice how items which we know are paid *quarterly* (like telephone, heat and light etc) are shown as *monthly* expenditures. This is not a mistake, the reason is as follows. Cash flow forecasts show income and expenditure as it actually happens. Profit forecasts on the other hand adjust income and expenditure to reflect the amounts incurred in the month even though the payment may not be due until the end of that quarter. This is rather surprising to some people; however it is entirely in line with the accounting treatment of 'accruals' and 'prepayments' which we covered in the first part of this book. You will see that each overhead amount has a percentage figure written alongside it. The key to calculating these percentages is shown on page 150.

Notice on the net profit line at the bottom of page 148 that some months actually show a loss. This is due to the seasonal nature of the business. Provided the profitable months outweigh the unprofitable months, this is not a problem for Bill and Ben.

Example 5 – Bill and Ben's Garden Centre

	ACTUAL 1994/95		ACTUAL 1995/96		BUDGET 1996/97		BUDGET BY MONTH											
							MAY	JUNE	JULY	AUGUST	SEPT.	OCT.	NOV.	DEC.	JAN.	FEB.	MARCH	APRIL
	£	%	£	%	£	%	£	£	£	£	£	£	£	£	£	£	£	£
GROSS PROFIT B/FWD	67000	38	85000	39	100500	38	16100	16920	12900	10560	7550	5620	4120	6870	2950	4240	6160	6510
VARIABLE OVERHEADS																		
Casual Staff Wages	13400	7	17000	7	20220	8	3220	3384	[illegible]	[illegible]	[illegible]	[illegible]	[illegible]	[illegible]	[illegible]	[illegible]	[illegible]	1422
Water Charges	2010	2	2550	2	3035	1	483	508	[illegible]	[illegible]	[illegible]	[illegible]	[illegible]	[illegible]	[illegible]	[illegible]	[illegible]	213
TOTAL VARIABLE O/HEADS	15410	9	19550	9	23255	9	3703	3892	2967	2429	1737	1293	948	1580	679	975	1417	1635
FIXED OVERHEADS																		
Rent	12000	7	12000	5	12000	4	1000	1000	1000	1000	1000	1000	1000	1000	1000	1000	1000	1000
Rates	6000	3	6600	3	7200	3	600	600	600	600	600	600	600	600	600	600	600	600
Light and Heat	4800	3	5200	2	5600	2	200	200	[illegible]	[illegible]	[illegible]	[illegible]	[illegible]	[illegible]	[illegible]	[illegible]	[illegible]	600
Salaries	5000	3	5500	3	6000	2	500	500	[illegible]	[illegible]	[illegible]	[illegible]	[illegible]	[illegible]	[illegible]	[illegible]	[illegible]	500
Stationery & advertising	2400	1	3600	2	4200	2	350	350	[illegible]	[illegible]	[illegible]	[illegible]	[illegible]	[illegible]	[illegible]	[illegible]	[illegible]	350
Motor expenses	1560	1	2100	1	2640	1	220	220	[illegible]	[illegible]	[illegible]	[illegible]	[illegible]	[illegible]	[illegible]	[illegible]	[illegible]	220
Telephone	900	1	1200	1	1620	1	135	135	135	135	135	135	135	135	135	135	135	135
Sundries	600	0	900	0	1200	0	100	100	100	100	100	100	100	100	100	100	100	100
TOTAL FIXED OVERHEADS	33260	19	37100	17	40460	15	3105	3105	3105	3105	3105	3305	3705	3705	3705	3505	3505	3505
NET PROFIT	18330	10	28350	13	36785	14	9292	9923	6828	5026	2708	1022	-533	1585	-1434	-240	1238	1370

Gross profit percent figure carried down from the trading account

All figures expressed as a percentage of total sales - £265,000.

eg Casual Staff Wages $\frac{20,220 \times 100}{265,000} = 8\%$

Now let us continue our profit budget for Playaway. Remember you completed the trading account on page 48. We will now complete the overheads section. To keep this simple, we have restricted the number of variables.

Exercise 16 Profit and Loss Budget for Playaway

We completed the trading budget for Playaway in Exercise 15 on page 146. We will now take the exercise one stage further and produce the profit and loss budget. You will remember that we calculated the gross profit figures for each month. These figures have been inserted for you on page 154 as the brought forward figures in this exercise.

We will now use the answer sheet on page 154 to calculate our variable overheads, fixed overheads and net profit for each month of the budget year. In this example, there is no need for departmental analysis. Let's start with variable overheads.

Variable Overheads We will assume that staff wages comprise 5% of sales. Calculate the total wages for the year based on the sales figures you worked out on page 143. Enter your annual staff wages budget in the Budget 1997 column. You then need to work out the monthly wages figure by taking 5% of each month's total sales. Ensure that the monthly figures add up to your total budget figure for the year.

Fixed Overheads Although these overheads are described as 'fixed', they will vary from year to year. For example some expenses will be increased by general inflation. Other expenses, such as rates, will be increased by factors totally outside your control.

Continued overleaf

Exercise 16 (Contd)

Shown below are the results of a fixed overheads review which you would normally undertake yourself.

1 Rent is fixed at £6,000 per annum.
2 The new rates bill is in hand and it is £400 more than 1996.
3 Light and heat is estimated to be 5% more than 1996.
4 Total office staff salaries have been increased by £300 per annum.
5 Advertising is to be double the 1996 figure.
6 Motor expenses are estimated at £200 per month.
7 Telephone is estimated at £40 per month.
8 Sundry expenses are estimated at £25 per month.

Enter all the above in your Budget 1997 column on page 154 and then split the total by month. We will assume that each month comprises one twelfth of the total fixed overheads amount.

When you have entered all the fixed overheads, you will be able to work out your projected annual net profit and monthly net profit figures. This is done as follows:

Gross Profit
less Variable Overheads
less Fixed Overheads
equals Net Profit

You have nearly completed your projection. There are still a few percentage calculations to do. Look at your worksheet and you will see that each fixed and variable expense was expressed as a percentage of sales for 1995 and 1996. Calculate your overhead percentages for your 1997 projection in a similar manner (these calculations are similar to the calculations you have worked out before). It is important to remember that your total budgeted sales were £115,700 and all your calculations will be based on that figure.

Continued

Exercise 16 (Contd)

As a guide, here is an example based on the staff wages for 1996. Staff wages for 1996 were £4,270. Total sales were £99,000. Therefore, staff wages as a percentage of sales would be:

$$\frac{£4270 \times 100}{£99000} = 4\%$$

Enter the budget percentages on your worksheet.

Obviously, if you add up all your percentages, they must come to 100%. Fill in your percentages for 1997 below and see if you are right!

	1995 %	1996 %	1997 %
Sales	100	100	100
Cost of Sales	57	56	
Variable Overheads	4	4	
Fixed Overheads	20	18	
Net Profit	19	22	
	100	100	100

You will note some calculations are shown as 0%. This is because we have taken the percentages to the nearest whole number. You can, of course, take the percentage to one or two decimal places if you wish.

Your profit projection for 1997 is now completed! Check and review all your entries. Compare your answer with that on page 189. If you have got it right – ***Congratulations!*** If you have made a few mistakes, review and correct your figures.

Exercise 17 – Playaway

Profit Forecast From May 1996 to April 1997

	ACTUAL 1994/95		ACTUAL 1995/96		BUDGET 1996/97		BUDGET BY MONTH MAY	JUN	JUL	AUG	SEP	OCT	NOV	DEC	JAN	FEB	MAR	APR
	£	%	£	%	£	%	£	£	£	£	£	£	£	£	£	£	£	£
GROSS PROFIT B/fwd	34000	43	42700	44	57005	49	3270	3270	3270	7449	3270	3270	3270	16855	3271	3270	3270	3270
VARIABLE OVERHEADS																		
Staff Wages	3400	4	4270	4														
FIXED OVERHEADS																		
Rent	6000	8	6000	6														
Rates	3000	4	3200	3														
Light and Heat	3000	4	3100	3														
Office Salaries	1250	2	1500	2														
Advertising	400	1	600	1														
Motor Expenses	1560	2	2080	2														
Telephone	200	1	350	1														
Sundries	150	0	225	0														
TOTAL FIXED OVERHEADS	15560	22	17055	18														
NET PROFIT	15040	19	21375	22														

You have now set your targets and you know what you want to achieve. In the coming months, you will be able to compare your actual trading results with your budget.

We recommend that you seriously consider computerising your accounting records. There are a number of excellent accounting packages available today at reasonable prices. These will enable you to enter your budget figures into the computer quickly. The computer will produce monthly 'actual' trading profit and loss accounts and compare these with your budgets. It will even calculate the variance between budget and actual, expressed as pounds and percentages as well! An example is shown on page 174 in Chapter 14.

Chapter 13

Key Management Reports

Most businesses have key areas of activity which warrant special attention. Often control of these key areas can make the difference between a profit and a loss. Key areas need close monitoring.

Key areas will vary from business to business but could include for example:

- sales performance
- control of debtors and creditors
- stock levels
- work-in-progress levels
- labour costs.

We will now look at several of these areas in more detail.

Sales

Sales is obviously one of the most important business statistics. We have seen that a relatively small change in sales can produce a significant increase or decrease in profit. Sales statistics may be made more meaningful if they are broken down into categories such as:

- sales by region
- sales by type of product
- sales by sales representative
- sales by industry sector.

You will normally want to examine part sales and future sales projections. Part when care has to be taken when sales are seasonal because a lack of preparation could lead to lost selling opportunities.

Stock Control

Holding stocks in any business is expensive. Stock holding involves the following costs:

- storage space (including heat and light)
- storekeepers' wages
- pilferage
- stock obsolescence
- insurance
- interest on money borrowed to pay for stock.

Don't hold too much stock!

Accurate sales forecasting helps to control stock levels. This is because you don't have to carry as much 'safety' (or reserve) stock to cover unexpected demand. This, in turn, helps you to manage your cash better.

Stock levels can either be controlled by manual or computer methods. Computerised stock control is likely to be more effective. Here is the reason.

Ideally your stock control programme should be part of an integrated accounts package. This means that your purchase ledger will update the stock ledger when new stock arrives. By the same token, your stock levels will be reduced when a sale is made via the computerised sales ledger. This way your stock levels are kept up to date automatically. Printed stock reports from the computer will help you to check your 'actual' stock against the recorded stock. If there is a difference, you will need to investigate why the difference occurred.

Differences will chiefly be caused by:

- theft
- wastage
- deliveries of stock not matching the purchase invoice
- sales and 'returns' not being recorded correctly.

If the differences are negative, you will have to write off the difference. This will appear on a separate report which tells you how much value has been lost over the period. Whatever the reason, active stock control can save money. The computer stock report will show both quantities and values which are used in your management reports.

If you have a manual system, you have to update stock records by hand. This takes so much time that it is unlikely to get done more than once a year.

Work-in-Progress

Some businesses have work-in-progress and some do not. What is work-in-progress? It is the cost of materials, labour and other costs tied up in work which you have not yet been able to charge to a customer. For example, imagine that Bill and Ben sell elaborate conservatories which take months to erect. Whilst the contract is proceeding, Bill and Ben will be incurring costs. These costs may not be charged to the customer until the job is finished. All the money tied up in part completed conservatories would be Bill and Ben's work-in-progress. The value of work-in-progress should be recorded and reports produced. Work-in-progress reports are valuable because:

- The value of work-in-progress should be included in the management accounts.

- You need to know the value of work-in-progress when the contract is completed. This can be compared with the sales invoice (or contract price) to determine whether a profit or a loss has been made on that particular contract.

- The value of work-in-progress will determine the level of progress payments from the customer (where appropriate). This will enhance cash flow.

- The value of work-in-progress will enable management to discuss progress with the staff who are responsible for the contract.

Work-in-progress can be recorded by computer or manually. The same principle applies to both methods but the computer will do the job more quickly and efficiently.

The method used by the computer to work out the value of work-in-progress is shown below, this package is normally called 'job costing'.

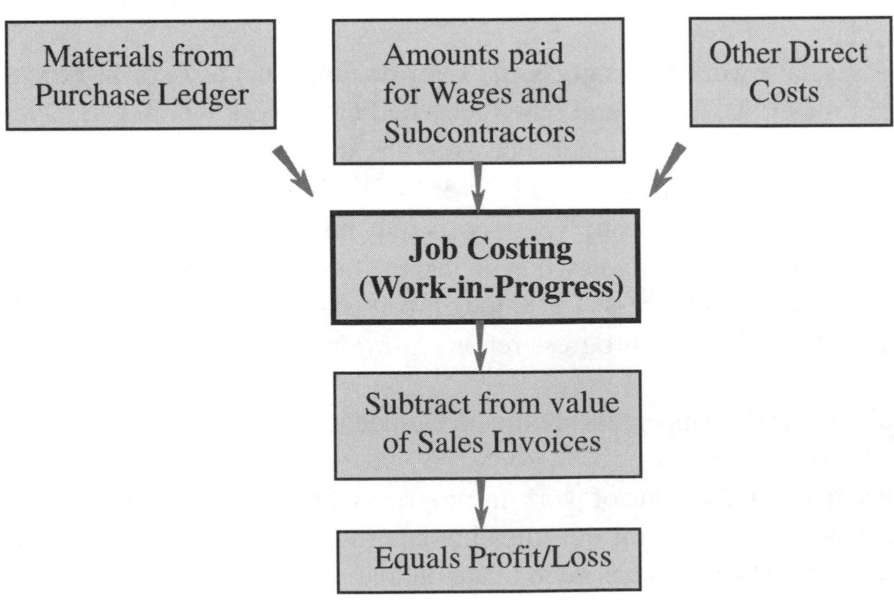

Controlling Debtors

All businesses need to know how much cash customers owe them. Debtors should be at a minimum so that cash flow inwards is at its maximum. Some customers delay paying their bills to improve their own cash flow. Most debts are unsecured. They can be a major part of your business assets; therefore it is essential that these debts are protected.

Collecting debt is a continuous process. It needs to be monitored closely and should include a regular review. Whether your system is manual or computerised, you should prepare a list of debtors frequently. Do this at least monthly, preferably more often. The debtors should be 'aged' into the categories below.

- Debt which is less than one month old
- Debt which is one month old
- Debt which is two months old
- Debt which is three months old
- Debt which is over three months old.

This is explained in more detail in the *How to Get Paid Promptly* book in this series.

A system of debt collection should be established and adhered to. Old debtors should be pursued rigorously to avoid the possibility of bad debt.

Your debtors control ledger will look as follows:

		£	£
	Debtors brought forward from previous month		5963
Add	Credit sales in the month		2427
			8390
Less	Cash received from customers	5012	
	Discounts allowed to customers	342	
	Credits given to customers	196	
			5550
	Debtors carried forward to next month		2840

Controlling Creditors

Every business needs to know how much it owes its suppliers. This will enable you to make the maximum use of credit available to you. The book-keeping procedures are similar to those used to control debtors. Here are the steps:

- Prepare a list of aged creditors as soon as possible after month end.
- Draw up a list of payments to be made from this list. All dates of payments should be examined so that the maximum period of credit is obtained.
- Statements received from suppliers should be reconciled (as suppliers sometimes make mistakes).
- Ensure that the delivery notes tie up with the invoices.
- Make the payments as required.

Chapter 14

Accounting Records

There is no point in making grandiose financial plans unless you can monitor your progress towards achieving those plans. Monitoring means that you need good accounting records. Your business needs an accounting system which is capable of delivering the 'actual' reports as quickly as possible after the end of each month.

There are two ways of keeping accounting records. These are:

- manual records
- computerised records.

As you will see later, we strongly recommend computerised record keeping. Let's have a look at the advantages and disadvantages of each method starting with manual records.

Manual Methods of Keeping Records

If you are keeping records manually, you are likely to be using either:

- An analysed cash book (probably along the lines of the methods suggested in another book in this series, *Simple Practical Book-keeping*), or
- Patent systems like Twinlock, Everite, Simplex etc.

If you are ***not*** using either of these systems, we suggest that you contemplate a change. We recommend that you take professional advice so that the new book-keeping system can be tailored to your needs. Let's look at each system in a little more detail.

Analysed Cash Book

If you intend to use cash flow forecasting as a basis of your financial control then an analysed cash book will work for you. Analysed cash books are very flexible so you can introduce whatever income and expenditure headings you choose. These headings should, of course, coincide exactly with your cash flow forecast. This is a major benefit. It gives you a co-ordinated system which really works.

If you intend to use profit budgets, you will need to keep extra books and files. These will give you enough information to calculate your profit 'actuals' (and also give you data for your key management reports). The following table lists these extra books and files and also indicates the kind of management information which each provides.

Note: Although we show the records and files needed to produce a profit figure, the labour involved is so great that you should really be considering a switch to computerised accounts if you seriously intend to plan and monitor profit. Hardware is now cheap and software is both cheap and reliable. The cost of installing a computerised accounting system will pay for itself many times over.

Record	Type of Information Available
Unpaid Sales Invoices File	Tells you how much debt is owed to you and the age of each debt. Tells you how much money will arrive and when.
Paid Sales Invoices File	Source of past sales statistics. Who ordered what, how much, and when.
Sales Day Book	This is a log of the two invoice files shown above. When kept, this should be a quicker source of information than going through files of invoices. Not all firms go to the trouble of maintaining a sales day book, however.
Sales Ledger Cards	These cards summarise each individual customer's debt. The cards tell you which customers owe you money and how long it has been owed. This enables the firm to get a better fix on exactly who will pay and when. The sales ledger cards also tell you which customers need chasing. Sales ledger cards are very time consuming to update so not all firms use them. If you have a lot of credit sales, you should use a computerised accounting system.
Unpaid Purchase Invoices File	If you add together all your unpaid purchase invoices, you know how much money you will have to pay out over the next few months.
Paid Purchase Invoices File	Tells you where your money has been spent on purchases. Add on your petty cash purchases to see where the remainder of your purchases money went.

Record	Type of Information Available
Wages Files	This tells you how much cash you have spent on staff. Don't forget to include employer's National Insurance contributions in your calculations since this is also a cost to the business.
Petty Cash Book	This is a source of spending on smaller items. The expenditure can either be analysed in the same manner as your main cash book or simply aggregated together as a single expense item called 'petty cash'.
Stock Records	You will need some records of 'stock' and 'work-in-progress' if you are to interpret the picture from your management accounts. If you are doing profit budgeting, you need figures for stock and work-in-progress to calculate your gross and net profit.
Other Records	You can obviously keep as many additional records as you think appropriate. Additional sources of management information could include a sales enquiries book, sales order book and goods despatched book. Also a purchases order book and a goods received book.

Patent Accounting Systems

These systems generally come in book form and incorporate weekly accounting records. Each book usually contains sufficient pages to cover one year. They include some form of pre-printed headings into which you slot your accounting data. These systems usually give examples at the front of the book to show you how they work. Patent systems tend to concentrate on the records which enable your accountant to prepare your annual accounts efficiently. They will not necessarily give you all of the information you need to generate your management accounts.

We prefer an analysed cash book because you are likely to end up in considerable difficulty if your business doesn't fit the headings shown in the pre-printed columns. If this happens, you will not then be able to produce good monthly management figures. Patent systems suit some businesses better than others.

Computerised Accounting Records

There are two areas where computers will help you keep records. These are:

- Spreadsheets
- Accounting packages.

Let's have a look at how each can benefit your business, starting with spreadsheets.

Spreadsheets

When you did the exercises on 'Trading Budgets and Cash Flow Forecasts', you probably felt that they took a lot of time and effort. To make matters worse, if you made an error it meant that you had to rework the figures manually.

The spreadsheet will eliminate this. A spreadsheet is a powerful computer programme which enables you to design reports – like cash flow forecasts and budget projections. Once you have designed your report, you will save an enormous amount of time and effort updating your figures. Each month a lot of your calculations will be done for you automatically.

A spreadsheet appears on your computer as a grid of rows and columns. See the example on page 68. The columns are usually identified by a letter and rows are usually identified by numbers. The grid creates boxes which are known as cells. Each cell can be identified by a letter and its corresponding number. For example, the first cell will be A1.

By way of example, have a look at Bill and Ben's Garden Centre profit forecast on page 169. This example was prepared on a spreadsheet.

Spreadsheets!

	A	B	C	D	E	F	G	H	I	J	K	L
1	**BILL & BEN GARDEN CENTRE - PROFIT FORECAST TO 30TH APRIL 1997**											
2												
3		**ACTUAL**		**ACTUAL**		**BUDGET**		**BY MONTH**				
4		**YEAR TO**		**YEAR TO**		**YEAR**		**MAY**	**JUNE**	**JULY**	**AUG**	**SEPT**
5		**30.04.95**		**30.04.96**		**30.04.97**						
6		**£**	**%**	**£**	**%**	**£**	**%**					
7	SALES											
8	**Department**											
9	1 PLANTS & SHRUBS	70000	39	85000	39	100000	39	20000	25000			
10	2 GARDEN FURNITURE	18000	10	22000	10	25000	9	5000	5000			
11	3 COMPOSTS	20000	11	23000	10	30000	11	5000	5000			
12	4 FERTILISERS	40000	22	50000	23	60000	23	10000	8000			
13	5 OTHER SALES	30000	17	40000	18	50000	18	4000	4000			
14	TOTAL SALES	178000	100	220000	100	265000	100	44000	47000			
15												
16	COST OF SALES											
17	**Department**											
18	1 PLANTS & SHRUBS	50000	71	59500	70	70000	70	14000	17500			
19	2 GARDEN FURNITURE	9000	50	11000	50	12500	50	2500	2500			
20	3 COMPOSTS	11000	55	12500	54	16800	56	2800	2800			
21	4 FERTILISERS	26000	65	32000	64	39600	66	6600	5280			
22	5 OTHER SALES	15000	50	20000	50	25000	50	2000	2000			
23	TOTAL COST OF SALES	111000	62	135000	61	163900	61	27900	30080			
24												
25	GROSS PROFIT											
26	**Department**											
27	1 PLANTS & SHRUBS	20000	29	25500	30	30000	30	6000	7500			
28	2 GARDEN FURNITURE	9000	50	11000	50	12500	50	2500	2500			
29	3 COMPOSTS	9000	45	10500	46	13200	44	2200	2200			
30	4 FERTILISERS	14000	35	18000	36	20400	34	3400	2720			
31	5 OTHER SALES	15000	50	20000	50	25000	50	2000	2000			
32												
33	TOTAL GROSS PROFIT	67000	38	85000	39	101100	38	16100	16920			

In each cell, you can enter words, numbers, or a formula. For example, a formula can be used to do additions, subtractions and to calculate differences, expressing them either as pounds or as percentages. The spreadsheet is a tool of infinite flexibility; it can even be used to automatically take data from your accounts package and reformat it to show the output on graphs, bar charts and tables. These may be easier to understand than the standard reports that your accounting package produces.

Accounting Packages

The cost of computers and accounting software has now fallen to the point that most businesses can easily afford to switch to computerised accounting. Depending upon the number of accounts staff that you employ, you could find that computerised accounting saves you time and money. The extra time saved can be devoted to other aspects of the business (like debt collecting!).

Although a lot of time and effort will be required to install a computerised accounting system, you will find the benefits are considerable. Initially you will probably opt for a period of parallel running using both manual and computerised book-keeping systems. However, once the system is established, you will find that the management information supplied in an accounts package is invaluable. It is important to get the installation right first time. Nobody wants to install an accounts package twice – once is quite enough!

There are many 'off the shelf' accountancy packages available at prices starting from around £50. Since you can't possibly hope to understand them all, you will need professional advice from your accountant or computer specialist on which package suits your business best.

Computerised book-keeping saves time and money, because entering one figure into the computer will trigger a series of related entries (like VAT) automatically. On a manual system, this takes much more time. Computerised accounting programmes normally comprise sales and purchase ledgers together with the nominal ledger which is the fulcrum of your management reporting. Other packages like stock control and payroll are available, if required.

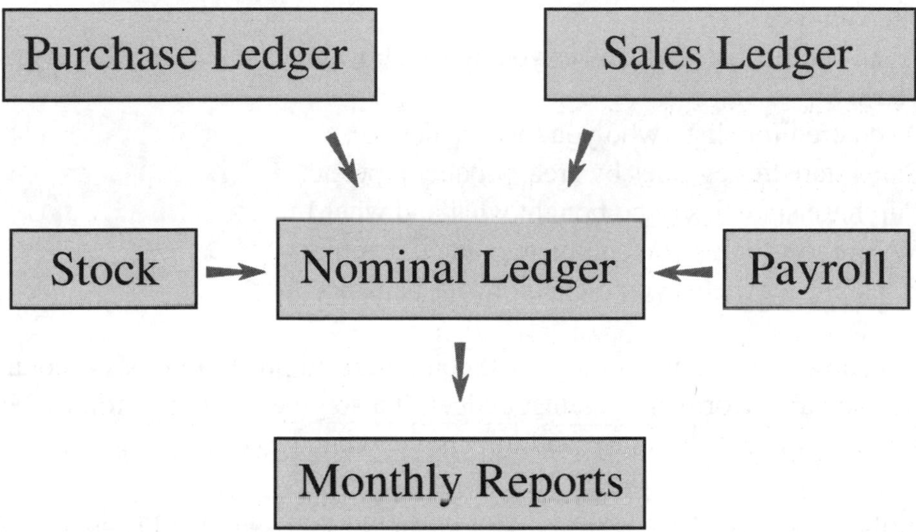

You will need to set up a chart of accounts, or a coding system, which will enable the computer to put the relevant entries to the correct accounts. Advice on how to do this is usually given by the suppliers of the accounting software or your accountant. Most accounting software has an in-built budget system which will give you monthly management figures. These can be used to compare your actuals with your budget. This will give you a variance between the two so that you can locate problem areas.

If you have not used computers before, we suggest that you obtain professional advice before installing an accounts programme. This is especially important if your book-keeping knowledge is sketchy. If you have staff with a good knowledge of both book-keeping and computers, you will find this helps the set-up process enormously.

If you haven't used accounting software before, don't be too despondent. Most packages include a tutorial which takes you step-by-step through the accounting package.

Once up and running, the computerised accounting system is a powerful source of management information. Here is just a selection of the information most accounting programmes make available.

- Profit and loss account.
- Balance sheet.
- Budget comparisons of forecast and actual performance, together with percentage variances.
- Aged debtors lists (who owes you money, how much and when they should pay you).
- Aged creditors list (who you owe money to).
- Sales statistics eg sales by area, product type etc.
- Purchase statistics (who bought what and when).
- VAT report (helps you complete your VAT return).
- Bank entries (helps you reconcile your bank account).

Page 174 shows an example of a typical computerised profit and loss account. This compares actual performance against budget. It also gives you the variance between budget and actual and shows expenditure as a percentage of sales.

Depending on the software you use, you may find you can also produce your own sales invoices, stock control, wages calculations and many other reports which will help you to control the business.

Even cheap accounting software is so sophisticated nowadays that the system will probably deliver whatever kind of management data you need. The more effort you put into understanding the programme, the greater the benefit you will enjoy.

If you move to computerised accounts, most of the manual 'books' cease to exist in physical form; they become part of a computerised database. The absence of these physical books can be a major blow if your computer is stolen or your database becomes corrupted. Make sure that you have a rigorous system of back-ups. That way a computer theft won't bring the business to its knees. There isn't space to go into more details of computerised accounting in this book. However, the topic is covered in another book in the series called *Accounting with Computers*.

Summary

- Before computerising your accounts, get professional advice on:
  - which accounting software package suits your business
  - which computer suits the software.
- Code your accounts carefully. This will enable you to get the full benefit from the system.
- Ensure that your staff receive adequate training.
- Have a rigorous system of back-ups.
- If successful, you will enjoy the following benefits:
  - know what your profit (or loss) is
  - know what your cash position is
  - know how much you are owed, and how much you owe others
  - know the total of your assets and liabilities
  - know what your business is worth
  - know how your current trading compares with this year's budget and past years' performance.
- You should be able to make decisions based on accurate, up-to-date accounts information.

Management Reports - Budget Report

	MONTHLY				YEAR-TO-DATE			
	Actual	Ratio(%)	Budget	Variance	Actual	Ratio(%)	Budget	Variance
SALES	52467.39	100.0	62500.00	-10032.61	84982.32	100.0	125000.00	-40017.68
Sales	52467.39	100.0	62500.00	-10032.61	84982.32	100.0	125000.00	-40017.68
Purchases & services	30366.35	57.9	41916.00	-11549.65	56068.58	66.0	83832.00	-27763.42
Carriage outwards	334.85	0.6	0.00	334.85	628.05	0.7	0.00	628.05
Purchases	30701.20	58.5	41916.00	-11214.80	56696.63	66.7	83832.00	-27135.37
	0.00	0.0	0.00	0.00	0.00	0.0	0.00	0.00
Gross Profit	21766.19	41.5	20584.00	1182.19	28285.69	33.3	41168.00	-12882.31
Salaries & wages	2553.36	4.9	2510.00	43.36	3841.52	4.5	5020.00	-1178.48
Rent	1270.50	2.4	635.00	635.50	1270.50	1.5	1270.00	0.50
Rates & water	-714.36	1.4	287.00	-1001.36	539.06	0.6	574.00	-34.94
Light & heat	190.00	0.4	0.00	190.00	176.75	0.2	175.00	1.75
Telephone	630.96	1.2	618.00	12.96	1052.69	1.2	1236.00	-183.31
Insurance	324.84	0.6	111.67	213.17	348.58	0.4	223.34	125.24
Motor & travelling expenses	1551.92	3.0	1589.00	-37.08	3832.28	4.5	3048.00	784.28
Accountancy & audit	500.00	0.9	250.00	250.00	500.00	0.6	500.00	0.00
Postage	88.00	0.2	50.00	38.00	88.00	0.1	100.00	-12.00
Printing & stationery	238.99	0.5	210.00	28.99	260.31	0.3	420.00	-159.69
Advertising	0.00	0.0	0.00	0.00	0.00	0.0	0.00	0.00
Lease of van	0.00	0.0	215.00	-215.00	0.00	0.0	430.00	-430.00
Car leasing	-150.41	0.3	0.00	-150.41	0.00	0.0	0.00	0.00
Repairs & renewals	0.00	0.0	300.00	-300.00	0.00	0.0	600.00	-600.00
Legal fees	0.00	0.0	0.00	0.00	0.00	0.0	0.00	0.00
Directors pension contribution	280.00	0.5	380.00	-100.00	560.00	0.7	760.00	-200.00
Sundry expenses	879.08	1.7	15.00	864.08	1171.43	1.4	30.00	1141.43
Bank charges	0.00	0.0	0.00	0.00	0.00	0.0	0.00	0.00
Bank interest	0.00	0.0	0.00	0.00	0.00	0.0	0.00	0.00
Hire purchase interest	-52.57	0.1	0.00	-52.57	-52.57	0.1	0.00	-52.57
Bad debts	201.76	0.4	500.00	-298.24	201.76	0.2	1000.00	-798.24
Bank interest received	0.00	0.0	150.00	-150.00	0.00	0.0	300.00	-300.00
Discounts allowed	162.27	0.3	0.00	162.27	653.46	0.8	0.00	653.46
Dividends	0.00	0.0	0.00	0.00	0.00	0.0	0.00	0.00
Directors Remuneration	8854.00	16.9	3950.00	4904.00	8854.00	10.4	7900.00	954.00
Directors National Insurance	903.12	1.7	0.00	903.12	903.12	1.1	0.00	903.12
Depreciation	650.00	1.2	0.00	650.00	650.00	0.8	0.00	650.00
Loss on disposal of asset	1904.00	3.6	0.00	1904.00	1904.00	2.2	0.00	1904.00
	20265.46	38.6	11770.67	8494.79	26754.89	31.5	23586.34	3168.55
Net Profit	1500.73	2.9	8813.33	-7312.60	1530.80	1.8	17581.66	-16050.86

Appendix 1

Model Answers

Exercise 1 (Pages 49–50) **Calculation of Sales**

Stage 1 – Adjustment for Credit Given

		£
	Cash received from sales in the year	70000
less	Sales debtors at 1 May 1995	(3000)
		67000
add	Sales debtors at the 30 April 1996	5000
	Sales adjusted for credit	72000

Stage 2 – Adjustment for Work-in-Progress

		£
	Sales (from Stage 1)	72000
less	Work-in-progress at 1 May 1995	(6500)
		65500
add	Work-in-progress at 30 April 1996	8200
	Sales per accounts	73700

Exercise 2 (Pages 51–52) **Purchases**

Stage 1 – Adjustment for Credit

		£
	Purchases paid for in the year	55000
less	Purchase creditors at 1 May 1995	(8000)
		47000
add	Purchase creditors at 30 April 1996	9200
	Purchases adjusted for credit	56200

Stage 2 – Adjustment for Stock Changes

		£
	Purchases (from Stage 1)	56200
add	Stock at 1 May 1995	5000
		61200
less	Stock at 30 April 1996	(6000)
	Purchases per accounts	55200

Exercise 3 (Page 53) **Prepayments**

The insurance premium was £2,400 which covered the period 1 November 1995 to 31 October 1996. This works out at £200 per month. Your year ends on 30 April 1996 – therefore, you have used six months of the premium and you have to carry forward a further six months:

6 x £200 = £1200

		£
	Prepayment carried forward from last year	900
Add	Insurance premium paid 1 Nov 95	2400
	Total	3300
Less	Prepayment c/fwd for period 1/5/96–31/10/96 (6 mths)	1200
	Insurance cost for year	2100

Exercise 4 (Pages 54–55) **Accruals**

(i) Your last electricity bill paid was to 28 February for £600. You have estimated what you will owe for the two further months to 30 April. By basing your accrual on the previous quarter's payment, you will take two thirds of £600, ie £400.

		£
(ii)	Electricity paid in year	2000
	less Accrual b/fd from last year at 1 May 1995	(100)
		1900
	add Accrual to 30 April 1996	400
	Amount to be charged to accounts	2300

Exercise 5 (Page 55) **Depreciation**

The van cost £3,600 and was expected to last six years.
Therefore, the depreciation will be £3,600 divided by 6, ie £600.

Profit and Loss Account for the year ended 30 April 1996 (Page 56)

		£	£
	Sales	73700	
Less	**Purchases**	55200	
	Gross Profit		18500
	Overheads		
	Insurance	2100	
	Electricity	2300	
	Depreciation	600	
			5000
	Net Profit		13500

Balance Sheet as at 30 April 1996 (Page 58)	£	£	£
Fixed Asset			
Freehold property	50000		
Van	3000		
			53000
Current Assets			
Stock	6000		
Work-in-progress	8200		
Sales debtors	5000		
Bank	12000		
Petty cash	100		
Prepayment	1200		
		32500	
Current Liabilities			
Purchase creditors	9200		
VAT creditor	2000		
Accruals	400		
		(11600)	
Net Current Assets			20900
Total Net Assets			73900
Represented by:			
Owners Capital			
Balance b/fwd from previous year	70000		
Net profit for the year	13500		
	83500		
Less Private drawings	9600		
Balance carried forward to next year			73900

Exercise 6 (Page 67) **John and Jean Gross Profitability Ratio**

	1996	**1995**
Turnover	303407	220519
Gross Profit	47090	46635
Gross Profit %	15.5%	21.1%

You can see that the turnover for 1996 has increased by £82,888 compared to 1995. However, the gross profit expressed in pounds is virtually the same. The gross profit % has dropped from 21.1% to 15.5% – a decrease of 5.6%. If the original gross profit % had been maintained, the 1996 profit would have been £64,019 which is an extra profit of nearly £17,000!

Reasons for this decrease in gross profitability could include:

- price increases from their suppliers
- failure to increase selling prices to customers
- theft of stock by staff or customers
- obsolete stock had to be sold off cheaply.

Exercise 7 (Page 68) **Net Profitability Ratios**

	1996	**1995**
Turnover	303407	220519
Net Profit	5222	13553
Net Profitability Ratio	1.7%	6.1%

You can see that the net profit is down by £8,331 in 1996 compared with 1995. The net profitability ratio is down by 4.4%. We need to look at the overhead expenses to see if there are any large variations. We can see that the total overhead expenses were £41,868 in 1994 compared to £33,082 in 1995.

In this instance, we can see that bad debts have increased from £722 to £10,283. Obviously, John and Jean have had a problem with bad customers! This illustrates that credit control is an area they will have to improve if they want to be profitable in 1997.

Exercise 8 (Pages 76–77) **Jack Jones The Butcher**

1 The gross profit margin for each year would be as follows:

Year ended 30 April 1995

Sales	51480
Cost of Sales	24180
Gross Profit	27300

Gross profit % is $\frac{27300}{51480} \times 100 = 53\%$

Year ended 30 April 1996

Sales	98294
Cost of Sales	38976
Gross Profit	59318

Gross profit % is $\frac{59318}{98294} \times 100 = 60\%$

2 The following comments should be made to the Inspector of Taxes on submission of the accounts.

Gross Profit Margin: During the year, Mr Jones expanded his trading operation by acquiring the lease of the premises next door and expanding his sales area into it. This has proved a successful expansion in terms of both turnover and the gross profit margin which has increased from 53% for the year ended 30 April 1995 to 60% for the year ended 30 April 1996.

Wages and National Insurance Contributions: We would comment that the overhead expenses in relation to wages and National Insurance contributions have increased during the year due to Mr Jones taking on additional staff in connection with the expansion of his trading activities.

Continued

Exercise 8 (Contd) (Pages 76–77)

Advertising: The expenditure for Mr Jones in relation to advertising has increased during the year as he engaged in an advertising campaign on local radio to convey the expansion of his business to the general public. This would appear to have beneficial consequences due to the increase in turnover and gross profit margin as commented on previously.

Motor Expenses: During the trading period, Mr Jones decided that it would be cheaper for him to obtain his stock direct from the wholesalers as opposed to relying on deliveries to the shop as previously. To facilitate this, Mr Jones purchased a new van during the year and the increase in the motor expenses reflects the additional costs in travelling to and from the wholesalers.
A comment may be applicable with regard to the increase in depreciation which would be due to Mr Jones purchasing the new van and, in all probability, due to additional capital items required in the new sales area, although this should be apparent to the Inspector from the capital allowances computation.

3 The following comments should accompany the submission of the accounts in relation to the Capital Account.

Capital Introduced: During the year, Mr Jones inherited £70,000 from the estate of his aunt. We would confirm that the capital introduced in the capital account is derived from these funds. If you require evidence to support this, we would be pleased to oblige.

Drawings: Mr Jones' drawings from the business reduced considerably during the trading period. This is primarily because Mr Jones wished to retain as much cash as possible in the business to facilitate the expansion of his trading activities. Therefore, he has been drawing from the capital received from his aunt's estate to supplement his normal drawings for living expenses.

Exercise 9 (Page 82) **Jack Jones The Butcher**

Tax Computation for the Year ended 30 April 1995

	£	£
Net profit per accounts for y/e 30 April 1995		14772
Add Back:		
Depreciation	6820	
Motor Expenses (20%)	207	
Entertaining	300	
Telephone (30%)	157	
Loss on sale of car	500	
		7984
	22756	
Deduct:		
Building Society Interest		2103
Adjusted profit for taxation purposes		20653

Exercise 10 (Page 96)

Key activities which might affect your cash flow could include the following:

1. Amount of raw material kept in stock.
2. Amount of work-in-progress at any time.
3. Amount of finished goods kept in stock.
4. Whether employees are paid weekly or monthly.
5. Amount of credit obtained from suppliers.
6. Period of credit allowed to customers.
7. Efficiency of debt collection.
8. How much is taken out of the business by the owners as dividends/drawings.
9. How well the business minimises its tax payments.
10. The amount of plant and equipment bought by the business.
11. The way the plant and equipment is bought (eg outright purchase, rent, lease).
12. The degree of borrowing that the business feels comfortable with.

Exercise 11 Pages 102 – 106

Cash Flow Forecast

ITEM	MONTH 1	MONTH 2	MONTH 3	MONTH 4	MONTH 5	MONTH 6	MONTH 7	MONTH 8	MONTH 9	MONTH 10	MONTH 11	MONTH 12	TOTAL
RECEIPTS													
Capital Introduced	2000												2000
Cash Sales	100	150	80	100	150	200	40	60	100	150	100	70	1300
Credit Sales		2200	3800	2600	1400	2200	3600	1200	1200	1700	2600	1600	24100
Sale of Assets								250					250
TOTAL RECEIPTS	2100	2350	3880	2700	1550	2400	3640	1510	1300	1850	2700	1670	27650
PAYMENTS													
Capital Expenditure	600			900	2000								3500
Cash Purchases	50	30		80	60				70	70		40	400
Credit Purchases		1400	1400	600	1000	800	1200	1300	900	900	700	1000	11200
Drawings	540	540	540	540	540	540	540	540	540	540	540	540	6480
NI	20	20	20	20	20	20	20	20	20	20	20	20	240
Gas/electricity			100			70			50			80	300
Telephone		30			50			30			40		150
Postage/Stationery		20		20		120		20		50		20	250
Car Tax		85											85
Car Insurance					135								135
Car Servicing				60				80					140
Petrol	35	35	35	35	35	35	35	35	35	35	35	35	420
Repairs/Maintenance	15	15	15	85	15	15	15	15	15	15	15	15	250
Business Insurances						450							450
Advertising	25	25	25	75	25	25	25	25	75	25	25	25	400
Professional fees		200											200
Loan Interest	50	50	50	50	50	50	50	50	50	50	50	50	600
TOTAL PAYMENTS	1335	2450	2185	2465	3930	2125	1885	2115	1755	1705	1425	1825	25200
Month's Surplus (Deficit)	765	(100)	1695	235	(2380)	275	1755	(605)	(455)	145	1275	(155)	2450
Opening Balance	-	765	665	2360	2595	215	490	2245	1640	1185	1330	2605	NIL
Closing Balance	765	665	2360	2595	215	490	2245	1640	1185	1330	2605	2450	2450

Exercise 12 Pages 109 – 111

Bill and Ben Garden Centre - Cash Flow Forecast Showing Budget, Actual and Variance Figures

	MAY			JUNE			JULY			AUGUST			SEPTEMBER			OCTOBER			NOVEMBER		
	BUD	ACT	VAR	BUD	ACT	VAR	BUD	ACT	VAR	BUD	ACT	VAR	BUD	ACT	VAR	BUD	ACT	VAR	BUD	ACT	VAR
RECEIPTS																					
Cash Sales	44000	46285	2285	47000	41690	-5310	34000	38245	4245	27000	28320	1320	19500	16120	-3380	14000	10233	-3767	10000	11449	1449
Other Trading Income	500	500	0	500	500	0	500	500	0	500	500	0	500	500	0	500	500	0	500	500	0
VAT Output Tax	7700	8100	400	8225	7296	-929	5950	6693	743	4725	4956	231	3413	2821	-592	2450	1791	-659	1750	2004	254
Capital Introduced	0	0	0	0	0	0	0	0	0	0	0	0	0	0	0	0	0	0	0	0	0
TOTALS (a)	52200	54885	2685	55725	49486	-6239	40450	45438	4988	32225	33776	1551	23413	19441	-3972	16950	12524	-4426	12250	13953	1703
PAYMENTS																					
Cash Purchases	27900	29655	1755	30080	28269	-1811	21100	26422	5322	16440	17190	750	11950	10320	-1630	8380	7495	-885	5880	6278	398
Wages & NIC	3720	3562	-158	3884	3824	-60	3080	3021	-59	2612	2826	214	2010	1919	-91	1624	1684	60	1324	1221	-130
Rates/Water/Rent	2083	2083	0	2108	2232	124	1987	2104	117	1917	1928	11	1827	1627	-200	1769	1616	-153	1724	1549	-175
Heat/Light/Power	0	0	0	0	0	0	600	960	360	0	0	0	0	0	0	800	752	-48	0	0	0
Repairs/Renewals	0	0	0	800	0	-800	0	0	0	0	548	548	260	0	-260	0	0	0	0	3259	3259
Equip/Hire/Lease	230	230	0	120	120	0	0	0	0	0	60	60	0	0	0	0	0	0	120	120	0
Insurance	0	0	0	0	0	0	0	0	0	2300	2520	220	0	0	0	0	0	0	0	0	0
Telephone	0	0	0	0	0	0	525	724	199	0	0	0	0	0	0	450	362	-88	0	0	0
Print/Stat/Advert	500	220	-280	400	329	-71	200	369	169	200	182	-18	200	262	62	200	149	-51	200	220	20
Motor & Travel	320	482	162	200	333	133	360	269	-91	300	292	-8	180	282	102	210	140	-70	140	189	49
Legal & Accountancy	0	0	0	0	0	0	0	0	0	0	0	0	2000	2000	0	0	0	0	0	0	0
Sundries	100	128	28	100	149	49	100	202	102	100	111	11	100	122	22	100	104	4	100	139	39
Bank Charges	130	130	0	0	0	0	0	0	0	240	240	0	0	0	0	0	0	0	150	150	0
Credit Card Charges	340	382	42	380	264	-116	260	302	42	210	225	15	130	109	-21	110	102	-8	100	162	62
Bank Interest	0	0	0	0	0	0	0	0	0	0	0	0	0	0	0	0	0	0	0	0	0
Loan Interest	200	200	0	200	200	0	200	200	0	200	200	0	200	200	0	200	200	0	200	200	0
VAT Input Tax	5084	5375	291	5548	5110	-438	4005	5066	1061	2982	3217	235	2571	2273	-298	1775	1575	-200	1127	1786	659
VAT Payable(-Refund)	2121	2121	0	0	0	0	0	0	0	7238	6538	-700	0	0	0	0	0	0	3275	2503	-772
Drawings/Tax	2000	2000	0	2000	2000	0	4250	4250	0	2000	2000	0	2000	2000	0	2000	2000	0	2000	2000	0
Life/Pensions Contrib	200	200	0	200	200	0	200	200	0	200	200	0	200	200	0	200	200	0	200	200	0
TOTAL PAYMENTS (b)	44928	46768	1840	46020	43030	-2990	36867	44089	7222	36939	38277	1338	23628	21314	-2314	17818	16379	-1439	16540	19976	3436
Net Cash Flow (a-b)	7272	8117	845	9705	6456	-3249	3583	1349	-2234	-4714	-4501	213	-215	-1873	-1658	-868	-3855	-2987	-4290	-6023	-1733
Opening Bank Balance	1050	1050	0	8322	9167	845	18027	15623	-2404	21610	16972	-4638	16896	12471	-4425	16681	10598	-6083	15813	6743	-9070
Closing Bank Balance	8322	9167	845	18027	15623	-2404	21610	16972	-4638	16896	12471	-4425	16681	10598	-6083	15813	6743	-9070	11523	720	-10803

Exercise 12 (Contd) Pages 109 – 111

Bill and Ben Garden Centre - Cash Flow Forecast Showing Budget, Actual and Variance Figures

	DECEMBER			JANUARY			FEBRUARY			MARCH			APRIL			TOTALS		
	BUD	ACT	VAR	BUD	ACT	VAR	BUD	ACT	VAR	BUD	ACT	VAR	BUD	ACT	VAR	BUD	ACT	VAR
RECEIPTS																		
Cash Sales	16500	9826	-6674	7500	6628	-872	11000	14380	3380	16000	18390	2390	18500	24625	6125	265000	266191	1191
Other Trading Income	500	500	0	500	500	0	500	500	0	500	500	0	500	500	0	6000	6000	0
VAT Output Tax	2888	1720	-1168	1313	1160	-153	1925	2517	592	2800	3218	418	3238	4309	1071	46377	46585	208
Capital Introduced	0	0	0	0	20000	20000	0	0	0	0	0	0	0	0	0	0	20000	20000
TOTALS (a)	19888	12046	-7842	9313	28288	18975	13425	17397	3972	19300	22108	2808	22238	29434	7196	317377	338776	21399
PAYMENTS																		
Cash Purchases	9630	9752	122	4550	4228	-322	6750	7333	573	9840	11230	1390	11390	14391	3001	163900	172563	8663
Wages & NIC	1874	1942	68	1090	976	-114	1348	1282	-66	1732	2004	272	1922	2239	317	26220	26500	280
Rates/Water/Rent	1806	1602	-204	1689	1436	-253	1727	1529	-198	1785	1926	141	1813	2007	194	22235	21639	-596
Heat/Light/Power	0	0	0	2400	1829	-571	0	0	0	0	0	0	1800	1426	-374	5600	4967	-633
Repairs/Renewals	0	0	0	0	0	0	400	0	-400	0	0	0	0	0	0	1460	3807	2347
Equip/Hire/Lease	0	0	0	30	30	0	0	0	0	0	0	0	0	0	0	500	560	60
Insurance	0	0	0	0	0	0	0	0	0	0	0	0	0	0	0	2300	2520	220
Telephone	0	0	0	320	440	120	0	0	0	0	0	0	325	293	-32	1620	1819	199
Print/Stat/Advert	800	1069	269	100	0	-100	100	0	-100	100	190	90	1200	1435	235	4200	4425	225
Motor & Travel	260	390	130	110	203	93	120	149	29	200	269	69	240	374	134	2640	3372	732
Legal & Accountancy	0	0	0	0	0	0	600	600	0	0	0	0	0	0	0	2600	2600	0
Sundries	100	148	48	100	179	79	100	124	24	100	118	18	100	155	55	1200	1679	479
Bank Charges	0	0	0	0	0	0	95	95	0	0	0	0	0	0	0	615	615	0
Credit Card Charges	145	129	-16	90	112	22	100	172	72	120	164	44	135	122	-13	2120	2245	125
Bank Interest	0	0	0	0	220	220	0	0	0	0	0	0	0	0	0	0	220	220
Loan Interest	200	200	0	200	200	0	200	200	0	200	200	0	200	200	0	2400	2400	0
VAT Input Tax	1888	1988	100	1332	1209	-123	1414	1436	22	1792	2066	274	2635	3163	528	32153	34264	2111
VAT Payable (-Refund)	0	0	0	0	0	0	1602	-100	-1702	0	0	0	0	0	0	14236	11062	-3174
Drawings/Tax	2000	2000	0	4625	4625	0	2000	2000	0	2000	2000	0	2000	2000	0	28875	28875	0
Life/Pensions Contrib	200	200	0	200	200	0	200	200	0	200	200	0	200	200	0	2400	2400	0
TOTAL PAYMENTS(b)	18903	19420	517	16836	15887	-949	16766	15020	-1746	18069	20367	2298	23960	28005	4045	317274	328532	11258
Net Cash Flow (a-b)	985	-7374	-8359	-7523	12401	19924	-3341	2377	5718	1231	1741	510	-1722	1429	3151	103	10244	10141
Opening Bank Balance	11523	720	-10803	12508	-6654	-19162	4985	5747	762	1644	8124	6480	2875	9865	6990	1050	1050	0
Closing Bank Balance	12508	-6654	-19162	4985	5747	762	1544	8124	6480	2875	9865	6990	1153	11294	10141	1153	11294	10141

Exercise 12 (Pages 109 – 111) **Bill and Ben Actuals**

Part 2

VAT calculation for quarter ended January 1996

	Nov	**Dec**	**Jan**	**Total**
Output VAT (Sales)	2004	1720	1160	4884
Input VAT (Purchases)	1786	1988	1210	(4984)
Total VAT payable 29 Feb 96				(100)

Part 3

1 Obviously Bill and Ben could not foresee the theft of the Christmas trees in December1995 and, as they were uninsured for the loss, this had a dramatic effect upon their cash flow position. The theft of the Christmas trees affected the overall sales figure. On the other hand, because they still had to pay for the trees, the actual cost of sales were in line with the budgeted figures. The result was a net cash flow deficit in the month of £7,374 which, when added to the bank balance from November of £720, left an overdrawn balance of £6,654 for the month of December.

2 We can see from the cash flow forecast that Bill and Ben introduced capital of £20,000 in January 1996. This capital introduced was drawn, in our example, from private sources. However, in many instances where an unpredicted event occurs, the business might need a loan or an overdraft from the bank. The introduction of the £20,000 corrected the overdrawn balance and, in January 1996, left a credit bank balance of £5,747.

3 Looking at the budgeted figures, Bill and Ben had obviously predicted the seasonal nature of the Garden Centre trade and had used their previous experience to predict the level of sales during the year and the associated costs.

Continued

Exercise 12 (Contd)

Overall total sales were slightly in advance of the budgeted figures, although only by £1,191. There is an obvious seasonal variation in the figures and there was a substantial variance in December due to the theft of Christmas trees. The total expenditure is in advance of the budget by £11,258 which, together with the only slight increase in budgeted turnover, would have led to a substantial cash deficit. However, the capital of £20,000 introduced by Bill and Ben rescued the cash position.

Exercise 14 (Page 135)

Double Sales:

Sales	200
Cost of Sales	80
Gross Profit	120
Overheads	30
Net Profit	90

Halve Sales:

Sales	50
Cost of Sales	20
Gross Profit	30
Overheads	30
Net Profit	Nil

Notice that:

(i) doubling the sales *trebles* the net profit.
(ii) halving the sales *eliminates* the net profit.

This example shows how sensitive profit can be. It is important to understand how changes in your business activity can affect your profit. These changes can be caused by selling more (or less), increasing (or reducing) prices, taking on extra overheads etc.

Exercise 15 – Playaway Pages 142 – 146

Trading Budget From May 1996 to April 1997

	ACTUAL 1994/95		ACTUAL 1995/96		BUDGET 1996/97		BUDGET BY MONTH MAY	JUN	JUL	AUG	SEP	OCT	NOV	DEC	JAN	FEB	MAR	APR
	£	%	£	%	£	%	£	£	£	£	£	£	£	£	£	£	£	£
SALES																		
Department																		
1 Toys	50000	63	65000	66	71500	62	3900	3900	3900	3900	3900	3900	3900	28600	3900	3900	3900	3900
2 Educational	30000	37	34000	34	44200	38	2813	2813	2813	13260	2813	2813	2813	2813	2813	2812	2812	2812
TOTAL	80000	100	99000	100	115700	100	6713	6713	6713	17160	6713	6713	6713	31413	6713	6712	6712	6712
COST OF SALES																		
Department																		
1 Toys	25000	50	32500	50	32175	45	1755	1755	1755	1755	1755	1755	1755	12870	1755	1755	1755	1755
2 Educational	21000	70	23800	70	26520	60	1688	1688	1688	7956	1688	1688	1688	1688	1687	1687	1687	1687
TOTAL	46000	57	56300	56	58695	51	3443	3443	3443	9711	3443	3443	3443	14558	3442	3442	3442	3442
GROSS PROFIT																		
Department																		
1 Toys	25000	50	32500	50	39325	55	2145	2145	2145	2145	2145	2145	2145	15730	2145	2145	2145	2145
2 Educational	9000	30	10200	30	17680	40	1125	1125	1125	5304	1125	1125	1125	1125	1126	1125	1125	1125
TOTAL	34000	43	42700	44	57005	49	3270	3270	3270	7449	3270	3270	3270	16855	3271	3270	3270	3270

Exercise 16 Pages 151 – 154

Profit Forecast From May 1996 to April 1997

	ACTUAL 1994/95		ACTUAL 1995/96		BUDGET 1996/97		BUDGET BY MONTH											
							MAY	JUN	JUL	AUG	SEP	OCT	NOV	DEC	JAN	FEB	MAR	APR
	£	%	£	%	£	%	£	£	£	£	£	£	£	£	£	£	£	£
GROSS PROFIT B/fwd	34000	43	42700	44	57005	49	3270	3270	3270	7449	3270	3270	3270	16855	3271	3270	3270	3270
VARIABLE OVERHEADS																		
Staff Wages	3400	4	4270	4	5785	5	336	336	336	858	336	336	336	1571	335	335	335	335
FIXED OVERHEADS																		
Rent	6000	8	6000	6	6000	5	500	500	500	500	500	500	500	500	500	500	500	500
Rates	3000	4	3200	3	3600	3	300	300	300	300	300	300	300	300	300	300	300	300
Light and Heat	3000	4	3100	3	3255	3	272	272	272	271	271	271	271	271	271	271	271	271
Office Salaries	1250	2	1500	2	1800	2	150	150	150	150	150	150	150	150	150	150	150	150
Advertising	400	1	600	1	1200	1	100	100	100	100	100	100	100	100	100	100	100	100
Motor Expenses	1560	2	2080	2	2400	2	200	200	200	200	200	200	200	200	200	200	200	200
Telephone	200	1	350	1	480	0	40	40	40	40	40	40	40	40	40	40	40	40
Sundries	150	0	225	0	300	0	25	25	25	25	25	25	25	25	25	25	25	25
TOTAL FIXED OVERHEADS	15560	22	17055	18	19035	16	1587	1587	1587	1586	1586	1586	1586	1586	1586	1586	1586	1586
NET PROFIT	15040	19	21375	22	32185	28	1347	1347	1347	5005	5005	1348	1348	13698	1350	1349	1349	1349

Appendix 2

Typical Gross Profit % Margins by Trade

Type of Trade	Gross Profit Margin as % of Sales
Antique Dealers	
Exclusive to trade	10 – 15%
Middle of the road dealer	30 – 40%
Bric-a-brac and books	45 – 50%
Bakeries	
Specialist, ie equipment and frozen dough	40 – 50%
Bakers who buy in all or part of stock	15 – 20%
Other – varying in range from	35 – 50%
Bookmakers	
Off course before taxes and levies	14 – 19%
On course	10%
Booksellers	30 – 45%
Building Supplies	
Cement/concrete/plaster	10 – 15%
Blocks/bricks	25 – 30%
Timber	25 – 30%
Sand/gravel	30%
Hardware	40%
Roofing materials	20 – 22%
To builders and other trades	25 – 28%
To retail customers	30 – 35%
Butchers	25%
Carpet Wholesalers	20 – 23%
Chandlers and Marine Suppliers	28 – 34%

Type of Trade	Gross Profit Margin as % of Sales
Chemists	
NHS dispensing	under 20%
Retail counter sales	28%
Chinese Restaurants and Takeaways	65%
Clothing Retailers	
Large multiple retailers	45%
Single outlet	37%
Computer Consultants	35 – 40%
Confectioners, Tobacconists and Newsagents	17%
Cycle Dealers	20 – 30%
Delicatessens	30 – 40%
DIY Retailers	25 – 40%
Electrical Retailers	
Including rental and servicing	18 – 25%
Excluding rental and servicing	25 – 35%
Fish and Chip Shops	
Takeaway sales only	40 – 50%
Including cafe sales	45 – 65%
Fishmongers	26 – 32%
Florists	45%
Footwear Shops	41%
Furniture Shops	40%
Garden Centres	35 – 50%
Greengrocers	18 – 35%
Grocers, General Stores and Post Offices	9 – 25%
Health Shops	30 – 36%
Hotel and Guest Houses	47 – 75%
Interior Designers	20 – 40%
Jewellers	33 – 50%
Leather and Travel Goods	44%
Licensed Trade	39 – 52%
Off Sales	9 – 23%
Mail Order	47%
Milk Retailers	34%

Type of Trade	**Gross Profit Margin as % of Sales**
Motor Accessory Shops	36 – 38%
Motor Trade	
Franchise dealers (paint and parts)	20 – 35%
Franchise dealers (new cars)	11 – 12½%
Used car dealers	5 – 10%
Off Licences	13 – 18%
Opticians	61 – 65%
Pet Shops	30 – 37%
Petrol Stations	11%
Photographic Equipment Dealers	15 – 20%
Printers	33%
Record and Music Shops	18 – 25%
Restaurants	45 – 65%
Riding Schools, Tack Shops etc	70 – 73%
Scrap Metal Merchants	24%
Shoe Repairers	83%
Toys, Cycles, Sports, Hobbies	32%
Veterinary Surgeons	
Small animal	77%
Mixed	70%
Large animal	59%
Video Shops	20%
Wool Shops	35 – 41%

Appendix 3

A Note on Value Added Tax (VAT)

VAT applies to goods and services provided by the business. The VAT rate will depend upon which goods and services are being provided. In general, we can identify three types of VAT. The first consists of VAT exempt items like most foods. The second consists of items which have a zero VAT rate like books, and the third consists of items which have the standard rate of VAT applied (17½%) like petrol.

When completing the cash flow forecast, it is important to know which VAT category your goods or services fall into. If the business is VAT registered, it will need to apply the correct rate of VAT to its sales. You will also need to differentiate between exempt, zero rated and standard rated supplies. The VAT charged on sales is called 'output tax'. VAT paid on purchases is called 'input tax'. You need to know which category various items of expenditure fall into. The following table may help.

Category	Examples	Rate
Exempt	Insurance Postal services Finance Education	No tax applies
Zero Rate	Food Children's clothes Books	Nil%
Standard Rate	Catering Adult clothing Footwear (In effect, any goods or services which are not in the previous categories)	17½%

Note: There are exceptions to each of these general guidelines.

VAT Fraction

Some invoices and receipts do not show the amount of VAT separately. This is particularly true in the case of small purchases from retail outlets. The formula for calculating the amount of VAT included in the total purchase price is:

$$\frac{\text{Rate of VAT}}{100 + \text{Rate of VAT}} = \text{Amount of VAT}$$

Assuming a standard rate of 17½%, the VAT fraction would be calculated as follows:

$$\frac{17.5}{100 + 17.5} = \frac{17.5}{117.5} = \frac{7}{47} \text{ of total invoice value}$$

The following example shows how to use the VAT fraction to calculate the amount of VAT contained in a VAT inclusive purchase of £117.50 assuming a VAT rate of 17.5%.

$$\frac{7}{47} \times £117.50 = \frac{822.50}{47} = £17.50 \text{ VAT charged}$$

If the VAT had been shown separately, the invoice would have read:

Sale of goods	£100.00
VAT @ 17½% of 100	17.50
Total invoice value	£117.50

Appendix 4

Work of the Accounting Standards Board

As you can imagine, accounting theory becomes as complicated as you want to make it. We hope the following notes will be useful for anybody thinking of taking accountancy study further. We said in our introduction that accounting rules are set by a body called the Accounting Standards Board. This is a committee comprising the six major accounting professional bodies in England, Scotland, Wales and Ireland. The aims of the Accounting Standards Board are to 'establish and improve standards of financial accounting and reporting for the benefit of users, preparers and auditors of financial information. The work of the Board is published and the outcomes are expressed in various forms. These include:

- Broad Statements of Accounting Principle

- Detailed statements of practice called Statutory Statements of Accounting Practice (SSAPs). There are currently 18 SSAPs giving guidance on all sorts of items ranging from Accounting for Value Added Tax through to Accounting for Pension Costs. Here is a list of the topics covered by SSAPs.

  Statements of Standard Accounting Practice

SSAP 1	Accounting for associated companies
SSAP 2	Disclosure of accounting policies
SSAP 3	Earnings per share
SSAP 4	Accounting for government grants
SSAP 5	Accounting for value added tax
SSAP 8	The treatment of taxation under the imputation system in the accounts of companies
SSAP 9	Stocks and long-term contracts
SSAP 12	Accounting for depreciation

SSAP 13 Accounting for research and development
SSAP 15 Accounting for deferred tax
SSAP 17 Accounting for post balance sheet events
SSAP 18 Accounting for contingencies
SSAP 19 Accounting for investment properties
SSAP 20 Foreign currency translation
SSAP 21 Accounting for leases and hire purchase contracts
Guidance Notes on SSAP21
SSAP 22 Accounting for goodwill
SSAP 24 Accounting for pension costs
SSAP 25 Segmental reporting

- Additional standards are laid down in Financial Reporting Standards (FRSs). These are more recent guidelines than SSAPs and sometimes replace them. Here is a list of current FRSs.

  Financial Reporting Standards
  FRS 1 Cash flow statements
  FRS 2 Accounting for subsidiary undertakings
  FRS 3 Reporting financial performance
  FRS 4 Capital instruments
  FRS 5 Reporting the substance of transactions
  FRS 6 Acquisitions and mergers
  FRS 7 Fair values in acquisition accounting
  FRS 8 Related party disclosures

- Other guidelines are issued including reports from the Urgent Issue Task Force (UITF) which 'plugs gaps' where existing standards may not wholy apply.

- Statements of Recommended Practice (SORPs) are developed in the public interest and set out current best accounting practice. The primary aims in issuing SORPs are to narrow the areas of difference in the accounting treatment of the matters with which they deal and to enhance the usefulness of published accounting information. SORPs are issued on subjects on which it is not considered appropriate to issue an accounting standard at that time.

If you want to go into more details of Accounting Standards, you should read *Accounting Standards* published by 'Accounting Books' which publishes text on behalf of the Institute of Chartered Accountants.

Exercising Accounting Judgement

In Britain there are thousands of businesses covering everything from heavy mining operators to the running of a pop group. Businesses cover a huge range of activities; it is not possible to have one single set of rules which applies to everyone. There has to be some leeway which recognises the differences in business life. This huge range of businesses means that accountants have to exercise judgements in the light of the business they are looking at. These judgements can have significant effects on the profitability as reported in the profit and loss account. Judgement is required in many areas but the following are the ones most likely to produce distortions:

- treatment of depreciation of fixed assets
- treatment of research and development expenditure
- treatment of expenditure on patents and trademarks
- methods of valuing stock and work-in-progress
- treatment of income and expenditure on long term contracts
- treatment of deferred taxation
- handling of hire purchase and instalment transactions
- handling of leasing and rental transactions
- conversion of foreign currencies
- treatment of repairs and renewals
- methods of consolidating results of different businesses
- treatment of warranties for products or services.

The method of treatment of these items (and others) can significantly distort profits reported by different businesses in the same industry and between the same business for different time periods. The accountant has to exercise judgement so as to produce a 'true and fair view' and a consistent view based on trying to apply the same rules of times against a background of changing economic circumstances.

Many of these activities are covered by guidelines contained in the standard statements of accounting practice or the financial reporting standards.

International Accounting Standards

The British Accounting Standards Board works towards harmonisation with internal accounting standards formulated by the International Accounting Standards Committee. Often compliance with a financial reporting standard automatically ensures compliance with international standards. When standards differ, it is possible to isolate the precise nature of the difference which helps you to know where you start.

Appendix 5

Glossary of Accounting Terms

Account A personal or impersonal record of one or more business transactions to enable a balance to be taken at any moment in time.

Accountancy The process of analysing, classifying and recording transactions and operations in terms of time, quantity and money.

Accounting Period The period for which financial accounts are customarily prepared.

Accounting System The day-to-day method by which transactions are recorded and, ultimately, appear in the financial accounts.

Accrual Accounting Recognition of revenues and costs in the accounts for the period in which they were earned or incurred rather than the period in which the cash is actually received or disbursed.

Advice Note See 'Delivery Note'.

Aged Analysis Usually used on a schedule of sales ledger balances to indicate the age of the balances (eg one month old, two months old, over six months etc).

Asset Goods, resources and property of all kinds belonging to a company, or to an individual, which are used in the business.

Balance Sheet A statement showing the assets and liabilities of any trading concern, at any particular moment in time.

Balancing the Books The periodical closing off and adjusting of all accounts in the ledger, in order to ascertain the profit or loss made during a period.

Bank Reconciliation A statement explaining the difference between the balance of an account reported by a bank and the account appearing in the books of the bank's client (see 'Reconciliation Statement').

Book-keeping The technique of keeping accounts – of recording in a regular, concise and accurate manner the business transactions of an entity in a set of books kept for the purpose.

Books of Account A set of books which records the business transactions of a firm or company etc (see 'Book-keeping').

Capital The finance supplied by the proprietors of a business in order to acquire the resources (assets) with which to operate.

Cash Book A book in which an account (record) is kept of all receipts and payments of money, by cash or cheque.

Cash Received Abstract A form showing the cash received from all sources for each working day of the week.

Close Off To transfer to the profit and loss account in the nominal ledger, from each account concerned, the amount itemised in the published profit and loss account so as to leave, as balances, only those which are included on the balance sheet.

Contra The matching of debits with credits or the setting off of one against the other (also known as 'netting off').

Control Account A memorandum account consisting of totals of all items debited or credited to a number of individual accounts in a ledger so that the total account may represent the individual accounts when drafting financial statements. Frequently used for sales and purchases ledgers and may be utilised to provide a means of control where one clerk writes up the individual accounts in a ledger and another independently maintains a control account for that ledger (also known as a 'total account').

Credit (noun) An entry on the right hand side of a ledger account.

Credit (verb) To 'credit' an account is to make an entry on the right hand side.

Credit Note Document sent to a person, firm, etc stating that their account is credited with the amount stated (eg when goods are returned by that person, firm etc or an allowance is made to that person, firm etc).

Creditor One to whom money is owed for goods, cash, services etc.

Creditors Ledger A book of account which records the personal side of all credit supplies of goods or services (also known as the 'bought ledger').

Current Assets That group of assets in a cash or near cash state (eg cash, debtors, stock).

Debit (noun) An entry on the left hand side of a ledger account.

Debit (verb) To 'debit' an account is to make an entry on the left hand side.

Debit Note	Document sent to a person, company etc stating that their account is debited with the amount stated (eg as for credit note when goods are returned due to some imperfection or to correct an overcharge).
Debtor	One who owes money for goods, cash, services supplied.
Debtors Ledger	A book of account which records the personal side of all sales, on credit, of goods or services (also known as the 'Sales Ledger').
Delivery Note	Note accompanying the delivery of goods or services ordered (sometimes known as the despatch or advice note).
Depreciation	The measure of the estimated loss in money value of a fixed asset owing to use, obsolescence or passage of time (see 'Amortisation').
Despatch Note	See 'Delivery Note'.
Discount	An allowance deducted from an invoice price, account etc.
Double-entry	Method of book-keeping in which two entries are made for each transaction in order to record the two aspects which every transaction has and to provide a means of proving the entries by balancing the ledgers in which each transaction is recorded.
Entry	The record of a transaction in a book of account.
Extended Trial Balance	An extension of the 'trial balance' to facilitate adjustments and closing entries for the purpose of preparing financial statements, and to allocate each balance to the profit and loss account or the balance sheet or to supporting summaries thereto (also known as 'Analysed Trial Balance').
Final Accounts	The profit and loss account, balance sheet and associated notes as agreed by the proprietor of the business.

Fixed Asset — An asset which is in permanent use within a business, eg land, buildings, furniture, plant, machinery etc.

Goodwill — 'Benefits arising from connection and reputation'. In the case of an established trade or business, it is the connection and advantages accruing to it. The goodwill of a business is frequently a most valuable asset but is not capable of accurate measurement.

Gross — A total without any deductions.

Grossing Up — The calculation of a gross figure from a net figure by adding back the deductions.

Imprest System — Method by which a fixed amount is advanced, and the expenditure from the amount at the end of the month or period reimbursed, so that the monthly or periodic balance remains the same (frequently used for petty cash floats).

Intangible Asset — Asset which is neither fixed nor current yet possesses value (eg goodwill).

Inventory — The stock-in-trade and work in progress of a business at any given time.

Invoice (noun) — A document showing the character, quantity, price, terms, nature of delivery and other particulars of goods sold or services rendered.

Invoice (verb) — The preparation and despatch of the 'invoice'.

Journal — Literally, the book containing an account of each day's transactions. Now used for the entry of those transactions which cannot be entered in the bought or sales day books or cash books.

Ledger A collection of accounts. The principal book of account in which the entries from all the other books are summarised, divided into cash book, bought ledger, sales ledger and nominal ledger.

Liabilities A term denoting the combined debts owed by a firm, company etc.

Liquidity The excess of cash or near cash assets over current liabilities.

Net The amount of any charge or cost after all deductions have been made.

Nominal Accounts Accounts for the income and expenses of a business.

Nominal Ledger Otherwise known as the impersonal or general ledger. The ledger which contains impersonal accounts.

Personal Account An account showing transactions with a particular person, firm or company, as distinct from a nominal account.

Petty Cash Book A book subsidiary to the cash book in which are recorded all small cash payments.

Posting The transfer of entries from the books of prime entry to their separate accounts in the ledgers.

Prepayment A payment made in the accounting period of which part or all relates to a future period.

Profit & Loss Account A summary of all revenue accounts showing, as its balance, the profit (or loss) for the accounting period.

Provisions Amounts written off or retained out of profits to provide for depreciation, renewals or diminution in value of assets, or retained to provide for any known liability of which the amount cannot be determined with accuracy.

Purchase (noun) — Any expense for goods or services supplied to the business.

Purchases Day Book — A book of prime entry used to list, analyse and summarise all purchases and services supplied on credit (also known as the 'Bought Day Book').

Reconciliation — A statement showing the process whereby the balances of two accounts, independently written up in respect of the same transactions, which, shown an apparent discrepancy, are brought into agreement. The most common reconciliation statement is that used to bring into agreement the cash book and bank statement balances (see 'Bank Reconciliation').

Reserves — Profits retained within the business.

Returns — Goods returned to the supplier because they are faulty, damaged or not what was ordered.

Revenue — Income received from any source.

Sales Day Book — A book of prime entry used to list, analyse and summarise all the invoices for credit sales transactions.

Sales Ledger — See 'Debtors Ledger'.

Statement (of account) — An account, periodically rendered, showing the amounts due by one person or firm to another. Generally, a statement contains only the dates and amounts of each invoice sent since the previous settlement.

Statutory Accounts — Accounts prepared in a form suitable for submission to the Registrar of Companies for filing.

Stock (in-trade) — Goods held for sale in the ordinary course of business.

Suspense Account A temporary account for a posting which requires further investigation (eg unexplained items in the bank statement).

Tangible Asset An asset which is either fixed or current.

Total Account See 'Control Account'.

Transfer An amount taken from one account and restated in another.

Trial Balance A summary listing of all the balances in the ledgers of a business to prove the arithmetical accuracy and the completion of the double entry.

Turnover Net sales, ie total sales less allowances.

Vouch The process of checking information in books of account to the original documentation.

Index